Shlomo Knoller

MOTIVATIONAL MARKETING

YOU BET IT'S PERSONAL!

Shlomo Knoller

MOTIVATIONAL MARKETING

YOU BET IT'S PERSONAL!

How I Sold Goods in Millions
to the Richest World Markets

Shlomo Knoller

MOTIVATIONAL
MARKETING
YOU BET IT'S PERSONAL!

Dekel Publishing House
www.dekelpublishing.com

North American rights by
Samuel Wachtman's Sons, Inc.

English translation:	Ada Lewinski
English editing:	Richard Reinprecht
Graphic design:	Giulio Venturi
Proof reading:	Pnina Ophir, Dory Morik

For information contact:

Dekel Publishing House
P.O. Box 6430, Tel Aviv
6106301, ISRAEL
Tel: +972 3506-3235
Fax: +972 3604-4627
Email: info@dekelpublishing.com

Samuel Wachtman's Sons, Inc.
2460 Garden Road, Suite C
Monterey, CA 93940, U.S.A.
Tel: 831 649-0669
Fax: 831 649-8007
Email: samuelwachtman@gmail.com

Table of Contents

Foreword by President Reuven Rivlin

Jerusalem, 14 Sivan 5776

June 20, 2016

Mr. Shlomo Knoller

Dear Shlomo,

I was so pleased to receive your book, ***Motivational Marketing***, which describes your life in an exciting manner and which enriches the readers, and interweaves your story with the story of the Israeli society and industry over many years, of which you were fortunate to be such a significant part in its formation.

The State of Israel is not like all other countries in the world. Her natural resources are poor, her economy is not based on oil, jungles, or infinite lakes. Even so, it is not so long since the State of Israel was established and we have already become world famous, as a world power rich in science, industry, and technology. The resources which we possess for this are our human resources which you and others like you represent in the most wonderful manner. Our only resources that we ever had, as you described so well in your book, are the way we strive to excellence, the passion for knowledge, and the readiness to work hard and diligently in order to get to results.

The title of your book, which surely was not chosen in vain, contains the essence of your existence as a person and a director, and, even more so, it shows the characteristics of your excellence over the years, excellence that is a product of creativity, intellect, consistency, and hard work.

Even though you represent yourself as belonging to Israel's past, your deeds place you in the heart of the flourishing present of the Israeli industry, and even more so, you influence, also through your book, the future generation. You are a role model for the young generation, which learns from you the secrets of creativity, originality, and excellence in the industrial area. I wish you and request you to continue to tell them your story. Let them take part in your internal vision that keeps you going, in your personal story—which is the story of our nation.

A fascinating book!

Sincerely and in appreciation,

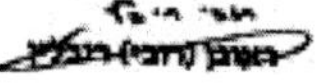

Reuven (Ruvi) Rivlin, Jerusalem.

Preface

At the beginning of 2012, following three years of indecision, I began writing this book in Hebrew and completed it within eight months' time. I was unsure whether it was worth it, but, on the other hand, I was driven to put in writing the story of my over fifty-year career, most of which as CEO and Marketing Director of manufacturing companies in Israel, the US, and the Netherlands.

With uncharacteristic modesty, I only wished to bring forth some of the knowledge I have accumulated over an extended period of managing enterprises that were taking their first steps or in a state of financial risk, which, through the right economic activity, have become—within just a few years—a success story. I wanted to demonstrate the manager's position when facing the market, owners, and employees, while the conduct was based on mutual goals and the yield was shared by the entire organization. I did my best to describe real life situations and present the stories in an accurate manner. In case I have offended anyone in the process, I sincerely and genuinely apologize.

The reader should bear in mind that, while Israel has meanwhile become a global hi-tech power with a strong and modern industry, in the first few decades after its birth in 1948, it had a small population of only 1-3 million, mostly newcomers from developing countries of the third world and holocaust survivors from Eastern Europe. Its export was minimal, mainly consisting of oranges and similar basic products.

This book is focused on the professional aspect of my life and therefore tells very little about my wife and daughters, but I must emphasize that the family that Edna and I created is the most important part of my life. Without this supportive family, I could not have been successful in my work.

We have been living in the Moshava (a type of Israeli village) Yokne'am since 1979 and own a 4-acre farm where we grow citrus fruit, pecans, and persimmons. Being able to combine my activity in the industrial world with agriculture has been a fabulous mixture that was made possible only by Edna, who took upon herself most of the agricultural burden including "manly" chores that involve driving our tractor.

I wish to thank Edna, my wife for over 60 years, for her support and the important part that she played in the writing of this book. I thank my friends for providing advice and critique, as well as our dedicated English translator, Ms. Ada Lewinski; the knowledgeable English-language editor, Mr. Richard Reinprecht and Zvi Dekel Morik, editor and publisher of Samuel Wachtman's Sons, Inc., Monterey, CA.

Shlomo Knoller

Yokne'am HaMoshava

Israel, December 2017

From Scratch

I was a member of Kibbutz Yiftach in Upper Galilee for five years (1953-1958); most of that time I was the manager (or as it was called at the time—coordinator) of the kibbutz's metal workshop and I also worked as the kibbutz's labor coordinator.

The Labor Coordinator designates member's jobs to cover all of the different workplaces throughout the kibbutz—both on the long term and on a daily basis—and is in charge of the occasional extraordinary work efforts ("recruitments"), such as the urgent seasonal harvesting of a certain crop. It is this person's responsibility to mobilize the entire workforce of members to make sure all that had to be done would be accomplished on time. It was considered a highly unpopular job as it would often result in clashes and quarrels with a great part of the member population.

The vote for the role of Labor Coordinator took place during an assembly meeting on a rainy Saturday evening. The kibbutz was of poor shape at the time, and the former coordinator, who was one of the veteran members, endured only two months in this role before resigning. The atmosphere in Chadar HaOchel, the public dining hall and center of social life where the assemblies were held once a week, was quite tense, and most members were angry about the sudden resignation. Two of the three candidates announced that they would not accept the job even if the majority would vote for them, and that they also did not agree on my candidacy. I knew that there was opposition to my appointment. The debate went on for three hours and was quite violent, including slanders and shouting. Speakers expressed resentment towards the resigning coordinator, as well as to the candidates for replacing him, while the stormy weather outside coincided with the storm inside. I just sat there in a corner and did not utter a word, as if what was going on had nothing to do with me. The Secretary-General chairing the assembly turned to the first candidate and thundered, above the roar of the storm, "Moshe, the kibbutz is in bad shape economically, if the members ask you to accept the role for six months, don't refuse." Moshe's reply was: "I will not agree under any circumstances, not even for one day." The same appeal by Secretary-General Yisha'ayahu to the next candidate, Pinhas, met with a similar reply: "There is no chance that I would agree." In the silence, Yisha'ayahu declared: "We are left with one candidate, Shlomo Knoller." All eyes turned to me. "Who is in favor?" Yisha'ayahu called, and announced, "Three for Knoller, who opposes?" and again announced, "two against, who abstains?" Seventy-five of the members raised their hands, and he announced, "Shlomo Knoller has been elected for the role of labor coordinator of Kibbutz Yiftach, for a period of six months."

Consequently, I was elected for this position four consecutive times over a period of two years, and I learned quite a lot from this job. I was very successful with meeting the needs of the kibbutz as an organization, but many members felt that I was too strict and initiated too many "assignments" to undesired jobs. I was considered a Yecke (Hebrew slang for a German descendent Jew, characterized as being orderly, rigid, and lacking a sense of humor) who did not take into account the wills and wishes of workers, and giving first priority to the workplace. Quite a few members even regretted their decision to abstain rather than oppose my candidacy during that assembly.

Getting Married with Edna

A year after assuming the role of Labor Coordinator, the Ministry of Agriculture informed us it had assigned a special budget for piping the entire Kadesh Valley area. About two months later, the blueprints were submitted, and within four months a piping contractor arrived at the kibbutz informing us that he won the tender and intended to start soon. He requested a go-to person from the kibbutz, and within a short time, I became his contact for any help he required, be it a tractor, a water tank, or any tool he might have needed. He provided me with a jeep and was willing to let me use it for the kibbutz's needs as well.

One day I drove to Ramot Naftaly, the neighboring kibbutz some ten minutes away, for a meeting. Passing by the kibbutz office and looking in, I noticed an unfamiliar young woman, so I asked the person I was meeting who she was. He told me that she was a Gar'in (a group, formed through a youth movement, of young adults intending to join a kibbutz) member, originally from the Moshava Yokne'am; she worked as a truck driver and sometimes lent a hand at the office. Well, a girl driving a truck was quite extraordinary at the time. There was no other in the entire Galilee area. I went in, introduced myself, and we talked for a while. Ever since that morning, I went over there each and every day…. A week after we first met, I asked if I could come to the shearing festival as her guest. I came driving the jeep, packing a pistol and wearing a keffiyeh (a traditional Arab headdress). We went together to the bonfire, where the festival was celebrated with singing and feasting on barbecued mutton.

When we went to her place to wash up, Edna hollered at me, "This is washing your hands? Haven't you heard of soap? Look, you ruined a towel." I did get a warning that she was a Yecke. At that moment I arrived at one of the most important conclusion of my life: I adored that gal! She was worthy of my courting and worth any effort. In spite of her hollering she was really nice. 'Next time I will do my best to overuse soap before I touch the towel, and if she agrees, I will marry her,' I thought. All this happened almost sixty years ago, and we have been together ever since. We enjoy each other's company, and I am confident it will continue to be so until the end of our days.

During the next three months, I would go to Edna's kibbutz right after the daily presentation of the work roster on the dining hall billboard. I introduced Edna to my parents in Tel-Aviv, as well as to my grandparents, who were thrilled to find out that she was a Yecke and spoke German. I was also introduced to her parents and all of her friends and neighbors at Yokne'am.

Several months later, we celebrated our wedding with 500 guests in Kibbutz Yiftach. We lived in the kibbutz for another year.

Edna headed the chicken incubator, and I went back to managing the metal workshop. Life was great, we were both glad to be a family, but we knew this was not our path. We were not thrilled with the communal life and wanted to rely on our own personal abilities to make a life for ourselves. Shortly after our leaving announcement, there were several attempts to convince us to stay, and some of the members even perceived us as traitors. But we were determined to venture into a new chapter of our lives.

Ramot HaShavim

A month before leaving the kibbutz, Edna and I went looking for a place to live. We hardly had any money (leaving the kibbutz, regardless of one's contribution while being a member, was considered high treason and you left with practically nothing.)

With great concern and many doubts, we hardly uttered a word during the bus ride to Kfar Sava, a small city then in Central Israel, in search of a place to start over. We were letting go of the good life in the kibbutz, our home, our friends, our social position, and leaving behind our secure life to step into the unknown. Was it the right thing to do?

In Kfar Sava, we saw two apartments that were not thrilling, got the cheapest available street food, a falafel, and went on to Kfar Warbourg, which we found to be a nice moshav, but above our means. From there we continued to the village of Ramot HaShavim, and really liked the place. The grocery store in the center of the village was immaculately clean and looked like my parents' place. It was quite empty, and an elderly couple sat at a table covered with a tablecloth and seemed to be having their four o'clock coffee break.

I started to explain what we were looking for, but they told us they didn't speak Hebrew. "Well," I replied in perfect German, "That is not a problem." The Heimanns gladly asked us to join them for coffee. They were a 60-year-old couple new to a land where people spoke a hard-to-learn language and tended to lack patience. They didn't have children to introduce into their home all that was local, and ran the grocery store in Ramot HaShavim as an isolated island of German culture.

Mrs. Heimann asked to hear the whole story, and we told her we were a young couple of twenty-three who had gotten married a year ago, had very little money, and were looking for a place to live and for work. We explained that Edna was a graduate of the Nahalal Agricultural School and I was a graduate of the Tel Aviv Shevach Vocational School and was an experienced metalworker. The Heimanns volunteered to inquire on our behalf, as everyone in Ramot HaShavim were their customers, and they promised to call us in one week's time, which they did, exactly as promised.

They arranged two meetings for me the following week. The first was with Mr. and Mrs. Avramson, who were both not in the best of health. They suggested that Edna would manage their chicken coop and that they would pay her a salary and let us live in their storage room (it was no palace, but it was reasonable as a starting point). I then proceeded to meet Mr. Hoffmann, who lived next to the small commercial center of the village and possessed a tin shed with cement flooring, about 6.5 ft. (2 m.). He was willing to let me rent it for the purpose of starting a metal workshop. On my way to the bus, I passed by the grocery store to inform the Heimann's of my achievements, gave Mrs. Heimann a kiss on the cheek, and returned a happy man to Kibbutz Yiftach.

When Ketos—the truck driver of the kibbutz—came to take us, I had already put out our few possessions: a table, bed, and two armchairs. We loaded it all on the Scania diesel truck and drove off. It was a gray dawn, everyone was still sleeping, and tears filled my eyes. I whispered to Edna, "I feel so sad, I will come back to visit only when we have a fancy car to park right at the dining hall's entrance, for all to see and envy."

When we arrived, and Ketos saw our place, he burst into laughter saying, "This is what you left the kibbutz for? Is this where you are going to live?" In a sad and quiet voice, I replied, "In five years' time we shall see who has the last laugh."

We set our modest belongings in our new living space and I headed to the shed that I had rented from Hoffmann with the tools I brought with me. I prepared a large sign saying: "European Grade Metal Workshop for Welding, Metalwork, Piping and Lattice. Best Quality and Credibility." I set up the sign and felt a surge of high hope.

Back at our living quarters, Edna had by then worked her miracles, and it became pleasant and livable. It was our first night away from the kibbutz. We had jobs and a place to rest our heads. The future seemed promising.

The next day we had our first breakfast in our new home and rushed to work. Edna collected eggs in the chicken coops, and I rode my bicycle to the workshop. First thing in the morning I walked into the office of the village's agricultural association next door, which appeared nice but modest. I knocked on the door and a voice from within said, "Please, come in." I entered the office of the association's CEO and presented myself as "the new neighbor." He immediately confirmed that he saw my sign and asked, "What are your credentials? Where do you come from? What experience do you have?" I told him I was from Kibbutz Yiftach, where I headed the metal workshop, that my mandatory army service was in the Pioneering Fighting Youth program, called Nachal, that I was a Shevach School graduate and that I had two years of experience working for the defense industry. I could tell that he was impressed with my background. He added, "I have already heard from Hoffmann about you renting his shed, and I also learned that our former maintenance person just left and we are in urgent need for a new one."

I offered to service the equipment and facilities communally owned by the moshava's agricultural association. I proposed a maintenance plan of routine upkeep that would require two days a week and offered to be available In case of any unexpected problems. I did not request employment and benefits, only to be paid for my services as long as they were content with my work.

The CEO was quite surprised, as this was not a conventional arrangement. He paused for a moment and then offered me a cup of coffee, which I accepted with thanks. When he came back with two cups, he said, "I understand what you are offering and it is interesting. Please name your price." While he was making the coffee, the fee I was considering had twice increased in my head.

I stalled while drinking my coffee, and then proposed two prices: a very high price for unexpected or emergency calls, and a lower price just for routine upkeep. The CEO was quiet, and after several minutes uttered in German, "This is a bit high."

We sat quietly for a few moments, and then I replied in German: "You are in control. If I prove to be great, you will want to further use my services, and if you are unsatisfied, you will simply stop." He looked me in the eyes and said, in German again, "We have a deal. Start tomorrow."

At the end of that day, Edna and I compared notes about our first day in our new place. Edna had fed the chickens and collected about two thousand eggs. I opened a metalwork shop and secured a job. We felt confident that we were on the right track.

Two days later a woman came to the shop requesting 20 cat traps. She was talking about a device that prevented cats from overturning the flowerpots. I inquired how much she paid in the past, and she told me that at a metal workshop in Ramatayim they were willing to make the devices for her but unwilling to paint them. I told her that for the same price, I would make them from better material and with any color of her choice. She asked me where I was born and when I said Berlin, in German, I seem to have won her over, and she placed an order for 30 units.

I later found out that this client was a central figure in Ramot HaShavim, and her good words got me about 250 work orders.

Mrs. Vera Sharon was another customer that I will always remember. She came in one day, sized me up, looked around and said, "Listen, young man, I have a 4-acre orchard, and fruit is being stolen from my trees on a daily basis. Rumor has it that you are a good but high priced professional. I urgently need a fence for my orchard, what would it cost me?"

We drove to the location and decided on the position and height of the fence, the location and design of the gates, and the materials. I rode my bike to my metal and hardware supplier, Mr. Bank, who also informed me that my customer was the mother of (Israel's future Prime Minister) Arik Sharon. I presented her with a price offer within a few days and offered to install the fence within two weeks. She negotiated the price, asking me to take twenty percent off my price. I agreed to drop ten percent, and she demanded a sixteen percent reduction. At that point I said, "Madam, a deal is a deal and it is either ten percent off or no deal at all. We can maybe meet some other time under different circumstances, but we will not do business together. This price is final!" When I got up to leave, Mrs. Sharon agreed to sign the work contract, and I started working.

After two weeks, I invited Mrs. Sharon to inspect the outcome. She carefully examined the fence, walked its entire length back and forth three times, opening and closing the gates. I could not believe her ability to run around like that in the scorching sun at her age. I literally admired her.

A week later I knocked on Mrs. Sharon's front door in Kfar Malal. She welcomed me enthusiastically.

"I am so glad to see you, and right on time as I have just finished baking this excellent cake."

She spent about half an hour talking about the cake and then talked some more about the tea, and when I tried to bring up the subject of money, she said, "We'll do it next Friday. I simply didn't have time to take care of it."

For several months I would come for cake and conversation every Friday (the cake was undoubtedly excellent). Arik Sharon, already a celebrated senior parachute commander, used to come every two weeks, and he would finish the rest of the cake in no time ..... Soon enough Mrs. Sharon started to trickle the installments, and the entire amount was paid within four months.

A new couple in their seventies, named Goldenberg, arrived from Frankfurt with no Hebrew and bought a modest home in Ramot HaShavim. Despite their age, they wanted to work, so they purchased a washing machine, two irons, a cart and a donkey, and offered laundry services. Twice a week, Mr. Goldenberg rode through the moshava, collected dirty laundry and later returned it clean and ironed. They lived a simple life and did quite well for themselves. The donkey, named Miriam, was very gentle and well behaved, and I found out that, except for twice a week, Miriam was available for hire. So three days a week I would load my autogenic welding equipment on the cart, go out to the fields and orchards and weld pipes. I would pay the Goldenbergs once a week and always made sure, as per their strict demand, to call the donkey Miriam, despite the fact that he was a male so that he did not get confused. . . .

We were doing well in Ramot HaShavim. I had a lot of work and was making decent money, the Avramsons were very pleased with Edna managing their chicken coop and paid her very well, we had friends and a good life, but we knew it was only temporary and that we needed to make long-term plans. I decided to look for a place where a new industry was forming, where it would be possible for us to live and work. Based on these criteria, I went to investigate the possibilities in the newly-built southern city of Ashdod.

The Rogosin Industries

Moving to Ashdod

The ride to Ashdod, a famous Mediterranean sea town since biblical times, took four hours (nowadays it is a 45-minute highway drive), and upon arrival I saw sand dunes on the Mediterranean shore, five apartment buildings under construction and about one hundred little temporary huts made of compressed cardboard material with no electricity or any other facilities. The huts were populated by new immigrants who had arrived three months earlier from Egypt and Morocco. The beauty of the place was breathtaking, and I immediately fell in love.

I walked to the beach that was almost empty, and the lifeguard invited me up to his tower for coffee and was interested to know what brought me to Ashdod. I told him about leaving the kibbutz, living in Ramot HaShavim and about our search for a place where I could start over and build a future for myself. He told me of a new factory that was in construction further along the sand dunes north of Wadi Lachish. He had heard that they were soon going to be hiring and that their offices were in Tel Aviv. I spent some more time talking to the lifeguard, and we parted as friends.

Rogosin Industries

I found out where the offices of Rogosin Industries were and a week later I showed up on the second floor of the Beit Ma'ariv, a building in Tel Aviv. The receptionist, an elderly lady, asked in an unpleasant tone of voice, "And what is it that you want mister?" It felt as if she considered me a nuisance. I explained that I was looking for employment in Ashdod and her response was, "We are not hiring as of now" and immediately added, "Good bye."

A voice from the next room hollered, "Geiger come in here, and who is it that you are talking to?" Without delay, I approached the door and saw an older man, over sixty (I was twenty-four at the time), who was astounded to see me standing there. After a long moment of silence he asked in German, "And what do you want?" I requested to come in. Mr. Gelber, the CEO invited me to take a seat, asked if anyone referred me to him and repeated his question about what it was that I wanted. I told him about my qualifications and experience having headed the metal workshop at the kibbutz for five years and about my own workshop in Ramot HaShavim, as well as my recent visit to Ashdod and our hope to live there, and explained that I was seeking employment in Ashdod. He listened and then asked me, in English, about my proficiency in the English language. I replied in English that I could read, write, and converse in that language.

He told me that they were in the process of building a factory for the manufacture of rayon tire fabric in Ashdod. He gave me directions to the location, seven kilometers north of Ashdod, in the dunes, and told me to go there after the weekend. He said that an engineer named Gilad would be expecting me and would interview me. He concluded by wishing me much success. Geiger, the receptionist and secretary, entered the room during our conversation and I could feel that if it were up to her, I would have been thrown out in no time.

From Ashdod, I walked for over an hour along a dirt track to meet with engineer Gilad. We discussed my experience, being a Shevach Vocational School graduate and the director of the metal workshop at Kibbutz Yiftach. He, too, asked me about the level of my English, and I said Mr. Gelber had already examined me during our meeting in Tel Aviv. He smiled and asked if we were related, to which I replied "kind of." He also asked if I had a driver's license and I confirmed that I was even licensed to drive a truck. Eventually, he wanted to know how soon I could start and we agreed that I would start at the beginning of the following month. I was to fit into the setting of infrastructure for the machinery that was to arrive from the US. The company was going to arrange for an apartment in Ashdod for us within three months, and until then I would be given a car and drive workers from central Israel back and forth. I shook Gilad's hand and told him he wouldn't be sorry for taking me aboard, and his reply was, "I am sure of it."

Back at Ramot HaShavim, Edna—who was already quite fed up with collecting eggs—was thrilled; and so was I. When I proposed to sell both my clientele and machinery to the owner of a metal workshop from Ramatayim, he was thrilled as well.

The CEO of the agricultural association at Ramot HaShavim was very sorry to hear that I was leaving in two weeks and offered to considerably improve the terms of our agreement, but I explained that my reasons were related to self-fulfillment. On the first day of the next month, I started working in Ashdod, at Rogosin Industries.

Working for Rogosin Industries

During the first three months, I drove every day to the factory and back with twelve other workers, and then Edna and I received a small second-floor apartment in Quarter A and were the first residents to move in. Ashdod was not yet connected to the power grid, but we considered our apartment a palace and rejoiced. There was no refrigerator, radio, or lighting, and most of the after dark life was centered around Mrs. Stephansky's hotel.

She had arrived in Ashdod four months before we did, got a building from the Ashdod Company that was erecting the city and opened a hotel. Anyone who arrived in Ashdod, engineers building the port and the power plants, specialists from Europe and the US, and the locals, all spent their evenings there. It was clean and good, the food and atmosphere sublime, Mrs. Stephansky knew everyone personally and she even organized singing and dancing nights. Everyone felt at home at the hotel.

Mr. Moshe Bremer, one of the best Israeli skilled professionals, was among the founders of Rogosin. He was a Holocaust survivor from the Netherlands who, after living for several years in Kibbutz Beit Ha'emek, was recruited by Mr. Gelber, a survivor himself, to be on the constructing team of the Ashdod factory, which was a move that secured the plant's technical success.

I became close with Mr. Bremer and was keen on learning from him. He was the only Israeli who was familiar with this kind of equipment, further to his work in Holland. After two months of hard work, we finalized the assembly of the infrastructure for twelve twisting machines, 28 yards each, which were to be the core of the plant. Mr. Bremer offered to meet me at the hotel that evening and confidently told me that this the management was contemplating three options: to bring in a foreman from a factory in Tennessee to instruct the local workforce, send an engineer for training in Tennessee, or send a company employee. Sending someone to train to be a foreman meant that person would spend four months getting to know the equipment and production procedures and processes. The goal was to bring the local factory on a par, as soon as possible, in terms of production times and yield. Mr. Bremer told me that he proposed to send me.

The first option, bringing in a foreman, was abandoned, as it had significant cost and partial efficiency, mainly due to a language barrier and acclimation difficulties. A job advertisement was then published in the Israeli press for an engineer that would spend six months in the US and then live and work in Ashdod for additional three years. After a month-long process, of which Bremer kept me informed, the management was left with two candidates and many doubts. They eventually decided to send me for a four-month internship in Tennessee. Prior to the final decision, Mr. Rogosin arrived in Israel and asked to meet me at the Tel Aviv Hilton. This was our first meeting. He inquired into every detail of my life and invited me to come to the Tennessee factory.

Ashdod was going through invigorated construction, the port was being built, and so was a new power plant. A direct road connecting the city to Tel Aviv was paved, and a year later the city was finally connected to power. We could leave behind the kerosene lamps and ice boxes, and listen to the radio. Edna and I started thinking of the possibility to come up with an amount of money that would enable us to buy a home in an upcoming suburban neighborhood.

I had a meeting with the local bank manager, who agreed to give us a loan, as did Rogosin Enterprise. After securing these loans, I also tried my luck with my grandfather. During our meeting in Tel Aviv, he interrogated me thoroughly, inquiring as to my salary and Edna's salary as a school secretary in Ashdod. He asked if I had tenure, what were our monthly expenses, and finally what was the amount we wished to borrow. I almost lost hope. He went on to inquire who else we had approached, and I told him that both the bank and my workplace had already agreed. He asked how much I was missing and I replied, "The amount that I requested to borrow from you." Grandpa was quiet for a while and then said, "Let me know your bank account number. The money will be in your account by next week."

This whole conversation took place in German as Grandpa did not know Hebrew nor did he wish to learn the language, as a matter of principle.

Managing in the United States, The Netherlands, Germany and Canada

The Journey to Tennessee

Edna drove me to the airport, I boarded a large airplane, and for eleven hours I mostly ate and slept. We landed in New York, the sheer size and height and the huge crowds were exciting. From there I boarded a plane to Tennessee, and upon my arrival I was met by a driver on behalf of Rogosin Enterprises holding a sign bearing my name. He took me to a charming boarding house, and I was welcomed by a nice little lady, about sixty, who showed me to one of the two rooms she was renting. The driver told me he would pick me up at nine o'clock the next morning. On our way to the plant we passed through a little village with a population of about a thousand people, set in a valley between two mountains. At about high noon, it all looked sunny, green, and bright—and this lasted for about two hours. During the rest of the time, the sun was behind either one of the mountains, and the valley turned damp, gray, and miserable.

The plant was initially owned by Germans and manufactured rayon (a fine fabric made of cellulose) tire fabric. During World War II, the American government seized factories that were controlled by the Germans, and Mr. Rogosin bought it from the government. Tires that were made with rayon could last almost 62,000 miles, while tires that were produced using cotton only lasted about 12,500 miles. During the war, the American army consumed millions of tires per year, the market was enormous, and purchasing the Tennessee plant had made Mr. Rogosin a multimillionaire. During my residency, the factory employed about 5,000 workers in three shifts.

When I arrived, I went to see the plant's production manager, who explained, in a heavy Tennessee accent, that I was to work for the next month with a team that assembled twisting machinery. He called the foreman, who told me that the factory would provide me with a bicycle and that I was to report to work every morning by seven a.m. After one month I would start working with a team of production workers. "I hope you learn something" he said, took me to the assembly area, and left.

I worked with the team every day, and to my surprise, no one talked to me. They would reply if I asked questions, but nobody asked me for my name or where I was from, and in the dining room not one person would sit next to me. I felt like an outcast and it really felt terrible. I asked Marjory, my landlady, if I looked funny, or maybe smelled bad, "Why do they all stay away from me?" She replied that they were checking me out and that if I am OK, it will be fine eventually. "All will be well, don't worry" she said, trying to comfort me.

I reported to her at the end of each workday and always received the same answer. I felt awful. This lasted for about a month. But then, one fine Thursday, the foreman approached me and said, "We all think that you are a good lad. On Saturday the team is going to Johnson City, and we want you to come with us."

I was thrilled. By the next day I no longer sat alone at lunch, and people even talked to me during the workday. The workers were all hillbillies. They lived in the mountain frontier areas, most of them had no more than four years of education, and they were backward and simple.

On Saturday morning the entire team arrived in a van to pick me up from Marjory's and called for me in a loud singing of my name. The foreman, in a suit and tie, took the steering wheel and was very friendly. We drove for about an hour to Johnson City, and on the outskirts of the city we came to a large building surrounded by vast parking lots. Above the wide doorway was a large sign indicating the opening date, which was that same day. We parked and walked to the entrance doors, where the foreman stood in front of the doors and called out in his thick Tennessee accent: "Open Sesame." To our surprise, the doors opened, and we applauded loudly as he stepped in. We each went through the same drill, and every time the door opened we all cheered. I was the last to go in, and then we repeated the same procedure on our way out.

We continued for few hours, and when we went back to the car I was really glad that it was over and that I had no acquaintances in Johnson City. The foreman gave me a hug and said, "Shlomo, I do hope you can drive. We are now going to have a bit to drink and you will take my place at the wheel on the way back."

When we arrived at the bar, it took me a while to realize what he meant by "a bit to drink." They were all intoxicated. Several of them lay outside on the ground. The foreman was the only one who was only half-drunk; he was only partially wasted, so he could help me drag my new friends and pile them up on the floor of the van. The journey back was silent. They were all passed out or asleep, including the foreman, who sat next to me. To my surprise, I found my way back quite easily. Back at the boarding house, I asked Marjory what to do with the bunch that was passed out in the van. She said, "Shlomo, this takes place almost every week. You are doing fine." She then called the wives of all my teammates, and each drove down from the mountains to drag their "crown jewels" back home.

During my four-month stay in Tennessee I surmounted social difficulties, played some basketball with my new friends, as they had a court there (some were taller than me, but being a former team member of the Hapo'el Tel Aviv team, I did quite well), mastered the work process of assembling interlacing machinery and operated the different production lines relating to all of the machines that were supposed to be shipped to Israel.

During my stay, Mr. Rogosin visited the factory twice, occupying the other room at Marjory's boarding house. He spent his free evenings there with me, invited me to have dinner with him, told me about the life of Jewish New Yorkers, and shared a little about his own life. At the end of that period we had a night of "having a bit to drink," and with great joy I returned home to Edna and to Ashdod. The America that I encountered was nothing like what I imagined or saw on the silver screen, but I learned a great deal and acquired many friends.

Assembly of the Machinery in the Factory

The machines started to come in from Tennessee one month after my return. We were well prepared with heavy machinery for hoisting and unloading. As containers arrived, we hauled them directly to their place and unloaded their content directly into position inside the production halls. Each 33-yard (30 meters) long twisting machine was first meticulously examined to meet Mr. Bremer's strict requirements, and the entire mounting process lasted about five laborious months of working from early morning to night time, all supervised by Mr. Bremer. When we were done, we set up for a festive opening, graced by the presence of Prime Minister Levi Eshkol.

Our plan for the big day was for me to turn the machinery on and have the factory up and going by seven thirty—at which time the CEO, Mr. Gelber, was to come in. The Prime Minster was due to arrive at 8:00 a.m. Geiger, the company secretary was supposed to pick me up from home by 6:00 a.m., and I was outside waiting for her ahead of time. She did not show up. Ever since my first encounter with her we disliked each other, but I never dreamed that she would dare pull such a dirty trick on me, leaving me behind in Ashdod so that the factory failed to operate on the day the Prime Minister was visiting. At 6:20 a.m. I grabbed my bicycle and got to the factory, about six miles away, as fast as I could.

I arrived only a few minutes before the CEO and saw Geiger's car parked up front. Entering through the back door, I immediately proceeded to turn on the machinery. By 7:45 a.m. the factory was operating in full, Mr. Gelber had arrived, and Geiger had already told him her story. She said that she came to pick me up at 6:00 a.m. as agreed, waited for me until 6:30 a.m., and sounded the car horn. She told him I was apparently still sleeping, that there was nobody, unfortunately, who could get the factory going. He was furious and shouted, "He will be fired without delay!"

The Prime Minister arrived on time, and when the CEO showed him into the production halls he was astounded to find the factory working. He showed Levi Eshkol each and every machine and explained the manufacturing process. When he walked by me, he couldn't resist asking me in German what had happened, and I only said, in German as well, "It is too bad that you have a bitch for a secretary," and moved aside.

Eshkol was impressed and complimented the CEO, and after he had left, loud voices were heard from the CEO's office. Geiger was not to be seen for an entire month after this incident. Mr. Gelber found an opportunity to say to me "I am sorry about all of this. I almost made a huge mistake."

The little town of Ashdod grew at an astonishing rate, and it became a city with Zvi Zilker as Mayor. The power plant offered many jobs, and additional factories opened near the port, resulting in a significant number of workers coming to live in Ashdod. Rogosin Enterprises worked in full capacity, supplying the complete consumption of both Israeli tire factories: Shimshon, in Petah Tikva, and Alliance, in Hadera.

I took a course in Industrial Management that was offered by the Tel Aviv University in collaboration with the Institute for Research into Production Efficiency. It was a trying and difficult period, through which I had to drive the company car to Tel Aviv twice and sometimes three times a week to study there in the afternoons from 3 to 7. Following my graduation I became Rogosin's production manager, and within a short time I also assumed responsibility for all negotiations and communications with the Shimshon and Alliance tire factories.

The Contract with ENKA – The Netherlands

Rogosin Enterprises signed a Knowledge Transfer Agreement with ENKA, a megacorporation under Dutch ownership, whose headquarters were in Arnhem. They supplied us with our raw material—rayon yarn for producing the fabric—and provided the knowledge and technology for production. The knowledge was transferred through Dutch representatives who would stay in Ashdod for two-week periods. Being the production manager,

I was their primary contact. Edna and I could communicate with them in German and English, we would invite them over, and our home became a home-away-from-home for them. We became friends and they spent most of their evenings with us.

Edna and I moved to our own private home, complete with a garden and backyard, in a new neighborhood mostly populated by the power plant employees. It was located only five minutes from the seashore by foot, so we went swimming almost every day, summer and winter, and I also took up tennis. At the end of that year, Edna gave birth to an adorable daughter who we named Michal.

We had many friends, our home was a social hub, and enjoyed our sweet, plump, blonde baby daughter. We felt great pride in our growing family and all that we had accomplished so far, and we made up our minds to visit Kibbutz Yiftach.

One weekend, as the CEO was away in Holland, I requested to borrow his car, a bright, red, large Opel. I felt like a king behind the wheel when we all set off in glorious weather that early Saturday morning from Ashdod. I never drove such an impressive car, and with Edna at my side and Michal in the back, I opened the windows and felt that even the music on the car radio was glorious. We were in heaven.

I parked the Opel next to the entrance of the kibbutz's dining hall, where no one could miss it as we went over to see Berale and Ilana. It was great to get together, and when we went together to have lunch at the dining hall, I could see from way back the gathering around the car. Mission accomplished!

Almost all the kibbutz members came up to greet us and shake our hands. Many also inquired about the cost, fuel efficiency, and performance of the car, in a nutshell; we really enjoyed the positive attention. At the time, people who left the kibbutz faced disapproving resentment, and if they did not do well also disrespect and even gloating. However, when successful, they would be met with appreciation and sometimes envy.

I told Edna they would probably talk about the Knoller family with respect and about the car with admiration for a while now. The truck driver, Ketos, saw us from afar and did not greet us. He surely remembered how he mocked us when we unloaded our few belongings in Ramot HaShavim and my words to him at the time, with tears in my eyes: "talk to me in five years . . . we'll see who has the last laugh. . . ."

Production Managing

The role of production manager included managing all technically related contacts with customers and with ENKA Corporation; overseeing quality control; securing orders and making sure they were filled out on time; dealing with any setbacks or complaints, and heading all relations with ENKA's engineers. I was charged with the smooth and efficient performance of the factory, led the large team that dealt with all of the day-to-day matters, but the overall responsibility was mine.

Four years into our alliance with ENKA Corporation, our exclusive raw material and knowledge provider, the corporation purchased its German competitor, Glanzstoff, and the consolidated company was named AKZO.

From then on, German engineers were sent to Ashdod to transfer technical knowledge, and German being my mother tongue, I was their contact in Rogosin. I flew over to the factories in Germany and the Netherlands, about once every quarter. I had many friends with whom I could confer, and I also learned a lot from comparing the methods and procedures in their factories with ours in Israel.

With time, my salary was raised considerably, and to the great delight of my family, I also received a company car. In June 1963 Edna gave birth to one more adorable daughter, whom we named Tamar.

Further to the collaboration with AKZO, we started implementing in Rogosin the newly acquired knowledge for the production of fabric from polyester. We were contemplating the purchase of a cutting edge dipping facility—a facility that enabled the dipping of about 550 yards—at the cost of about five million dollars.

At the end of that year, Mr. Gelber, the CEO, resigned and it was a great loss, as he excelled at management and was also an extraordinary human being whom we cherished. Mr. Rogosin appointed his nephew, Mr. Stern, as the new CEO.

A New Yorker and Yeshiva graduate who lacked any managerial experience and was condescending, he had no knowledge of labor relationships and did not know how to conduct his dealings with workers, especially unionized workers who worked with worker's committees. He was smart and quick to learn, but there were some issues that he never grasped. It was a very volatile period regarding labor relationship, the Ashdod Port workers were repeatedly on strike, almost every month, and all of the different worker's committees became quite militant. From day one, Stern attempted to establish his autonomy, communicating his approach, which was in the line of "You do your jobs, get paid, and don't interfere with my decisions."

Turmoil was unavoidable under these conditions. I did my best to guide him and advised him to refrain from the open voicing of anything that crossed his mind, but he only replied, "You have a lot of work—stick to your job."

During Mr. Gelber's time as CEO, the management-labor relationship was calm, and everyone had the factory's best interest in mind. Stern appointed another relative of his as human resource manager but did not delegate any powers or authorities to him. Within one year, clashes and confrontations with the workers were constant and endless.

By the end of the year, it was time for new labor contracts. During three months of lengthy discussions, the factory met with repeated short strikes and much disorder. When the collective agreement was finally signed, Mr. Stern decided to add a high-priced new facility for the production of Nylon Yarn. He also decided on a new hierarchical structure, where the factory manager reported to the CEO and the production manager—Shlomo Knoller—was subordinate to the factory manager.

I was furious. Rumor had it that the job was offered to the director of the Acrilan Plant, Mr. Matouk, for whom I had respect as an accomplished and experienced manager. At the time, however, I had completed eight years as production manager, and in fact it was I who was managing the plant. The fact that he did not even consider me for the position was quite a blow.

I conducted a harsh meeting with Mr. Stern and accused him of being ungrateful. I indicated that since my first day in Rogosin I had played a key role in its success as was evident from my relationship with both customers and suppliers of knowledge, who all revered Rogosin. He agreed with me and added that he was uncomfortable with my being too intimate with the workers and having a good relationship with the worker's committee. He concluded: "This is my final decision. If you don't agree, we will part." The Chairman (who was also a member of the Rogosin family and who knew me well) instructed the CEO to wait for his arrival in Israel the following week.

Proposal for a New Position

The CEO and Chairman discussed matters for a couple of days and then invited me to join the discussions about the prospect of building a dipping facility in Rogosin. After deliberating for an entire day, the final decision was to go ahead with this project, and it was agreed that I would take it upon myself to direct it for one year.

This position required traveling the world to visit facilities that had links with AKZO, as well as with DuPont. The first phase required trips to Europe and to a couple of facilities in the US. The second phase required me to submit a full report, to recommend the production and operation method (i.e., heated with gas, diesel, etc.), and I was also entrusted with negotiating with the selected supplier. We needed a dipping facility featuring two or three 33-yard towers, fit for dipping about 550 yards of fabric. The facility in question was enormous, and arriving at a decision would require at least a year. An investment of this magnitude was necessary for maintaining Rogosin's competitiveness and survival in the global and local tire markets for years to come. It was required in particular for maintaining Rogosin's predominance in the domestic market, since Alliance (who had purchased Shimshon) was said to have been showing an interest in buying a dipping facility. As there was no room for two such facilities in the Israeli small market, there was no question that for Rogosin to survive, building such a facility was essential.

If I wished to depart with Rogosin after the project was finalized, per the CEO's proposal I would receive a bonus equal to my salary during the last six months. I requested three days to think it over. The advantages were immense: an exciting and responsible job and a chance to become one of the world's experts in tire fabrics. Traveling the world would also be an excellent opportunity to see how it was done in Europe and the US, become experienced in operating different kinds of machinery and methods, and get to know and become acquainted with knowledgeable professionals and managers from around the world.

The only downside was that Edna was pregnant again and it would not be easy for her with three kids and me away for weeks on end. It is my good fortune though to be married to a wife who had always been—and still is—great support. I could, therefore, accept the offer.

We decided that I would show Matouk, the new manager, the customary ways things were done; and only then would I start my new project with the first two-week visit to Glanzstoff, which had been transferring knowledge to us for a full year by then.

Everything worked according to plan. I taught Matouk the work process and introduced him to the various significant characters, including the workers' committee. He was experienced and knowledgeable, and I expected him to learn all the details in no time. On the other hand, I was quite certain that he would not have the composure to deal with the workers, and I predicted that, in return, the workers' committee would spite him.

At the beginning of January 1964 I flew over to Germany, where work plans, as well as a nice little hotel not far from the factory, were ready for me. Being fluent in German and having visited Glanzstoff before, it almost felt at home.

The Dipping Facility in Glanzstoff, Germany

The fabric coating process used in the dipping facility involved coating with solutions that allowed for adhesion of the fabric on rubber. The heat and tension stretched the fabric and created properties such as flexibility and adhesion power. About 550 yards of fabric were spread in the facility at a speed of about 65 yards per minute. The shift supervisor at the command table set the process gauges according to specifications received from the laboratory and monitors, with the help of four shift workers, the required temperature, pressure, and elongating as per the technology page. I realized that the Glanzstoff plant was located in an enormous red-brick building which I calculated to have been built at great cost.

The manager, Mr. Taichman, was very friendly and prepared for me a complete training program that would also include working with the shift workers through the different steps of the process, then working next to the shift supervisors and, as soon as the shift supervisors approved of my capability, taking over the shift managing responsibilities. During my training, the relevant shift supervisors submitted, every week, a written report detailing my performance, grading it and describing my progress. Mr. Taichman conducted an official meeting with me twice a week, he always showed an interest in my well-being and together we read all the reports. During the final month, when I became the shift supervisor, the reports were provided by his deputy, Joachim, who joined these meetings. When I arrived in Germany, I had no knowledge of the dipping process, and within three months I was able to head the production process of the facility. I was confident that my upbringing and my knowledge of the German language were powerful tools that allowed for my success.

A month later I went to the Netherlands to train at Akzo's plant in Arnhem. It was a similar facility to the one in Germany, except it processed polyester, so it had three stretching towers instead of two, and the procedure was slightly different. I stayed there about six weeks and studied the production methods until I was fully qualified to independently operate their facility.

The Canadian Facility

About a month later I went to Ontario, Canada, where I learned to run an innovative dipping facility, based on American technology, in one of ten factories named U.S. Rubber.

The Canadian plant was entirely different, with another system for preparing the solution and a unique structure. The Canadians had built a solid base to which they attached the entire facility, including the 27-yard towers. When they were done, they erected a frame of steel rods and closed it with asbestos slabs. This structural solution must have saved them, according to my estimation, about four million dollars.

I spent my first two weeks in Canada training for the job of shift supervisor, and then replaced one of their shift supervisors, who took a month off during my stay. At the end of my time there, the factory manager asked me if I would be interested in staying in Canada as their employee, but I declined, of course. On one occasion, the factory manager invited me to spend the weekend at his house with his family. I accepted, gladly, as my weekends at the motel, in the Canadian vicious weather (it was minus 13°F = minus 25°C outside), were boring and lonely.

He lived in a big house, in a small village about thirty minutes from the plant, and the entire family welcomed me—his wife, two children, father, and most significantly, his mother. While I shook his wife's hand, kissed the children, and shook his father's hand, I heard his mother asking in German, "Hans, where is this guest from?" He replied in German that I was from Israel and she replied, still in German, "He is a Jew!" Hans turned to her and said, "This is none of your business, and this kind of babbling is inappropriate at your age. It is too much so, please leave now and go to your room." His mother proceeded to utter, as she was leaving: "You are young and foolish, the Jews are dangerous." I spent a great long weekend at their home. I had fun with the kids, drank some schnapps with Hans's father while we played chess, and discussed with Hans and his wife the situation in Israel compared to Canada while we were having some more of the schnapps.

The only one who stayed away was Hans's mother. Even at the table she only spoke German and never talked to me. She had no idea that I was fluent in German and she made remarks about me being dangerous because I was a Jew. The next day, when we launched another game of chess, Hans's father proudly put out his home-made cherry schnapps and said to his wife:

"Woman, why don't you bring over some of your cheese pastry so that our guest may realize that you are capable of doing some good?"

He translated his words into English for me. She brought over two plates and gave us each a plate. Her pastry was identical to what my grandmother used to bake. He said to her in German, "I am consistently losing in our chess games. Maybe my schnapps will help me win at least once." He translated this as well into English. I thanked her and praised her cooking in English. She had her husband ask me if I was married and had children, I could have answered her right away in German, but decided not to expose myself as of yet.

That weekend was great, and when Hans was ready to take me back to the motel, his father hugged me and said, "You are a wonderful man. I would love to meet with you again." I kissed the children goodbye, parted with Hans's wife, and finally shook his mother's hand and said in German, in a Berlin accent, "Do you still consider me dangerous?" She was shocked, turned bright red and said, "You are a German! You speak like one who was born in Germany. I can't believe it. You understood everything." She sat down, hardly breathing and murmured, "How did this happen to me ...".

I told her, in German, "Never mind, what matters is that you make the most excellent pastry, almost as good as my grandmother's."

The next morning Hans told me his mother would never forget me. He handed me a box and told me that after a sleepless night his mother got up early in the morning to bake some more of her cheese pastry for me. I too enjoyed your visit immensely he said, and shall never forget you.

Back Home

After each trip, I would compile a full report to sum up everything I learned and evaluate the advantages and disadvantages of the methods I encountered, and then prepare for the next trip. When I came back from Canada, I had two more trips to make before my final recommendation.

In the meantime, the factory went through several transitions. The chairman resigned, and Izzy Gilad replaced him. He was raised in England, had a degree in Economy and experience as a civil servant. On top of it all, he was a really good person. He introduced orderly working procedures: meetings started right on time, participants received the agenda ahead of time and a report the next day. I was very pleased to work with him, and I trusted his judgment. CEO Stern, on the other hand, was not too pleased, and apparently they did not see eye to eye on many subjects. Mr. Matouk, the factory manager, resigned for several reasons: his only supporter was the CEO, the workers' committee gave him a very hard time and did their best to make his life difficult, and finally he was aging and got fed up.

Eliyahu, a young man of Persian descent who headed the workers' committee, was a natural leader of his fellow workers, and he declared sanctions and labor disputes again and again in response to every small disagreement. The labor clashes in the port had an impact on the entire workforce at the time, and the situation in Rogosin was bad.

I put myself up for the position of factory manager instead of Matouk, but there was some opposition to my candidacy. The CEO objected to my labor relationship inclination and preferred a firm line even at the cost of strikes. The head of the daily rate workers' committee disapproved, since he thought I would turn the monthly rate workers' committee against him (which I would have). In short, there was a lot going on and no resolutions, but Izzy Gilad promised me to support my candidacy after I finalized the dipping facility project.

Within three months we had successfully deployed the dipping facility, and now, instead of selling fabric as a raw material, we sold dipped fabric. We purchased knowledge from General Tires, and Rogosin became an esteemed supplier, in Israel and around the world.

The relationship between Mr. Stern and the workers was on the brink of a full-blown crisis. The CEO thought he should teach the workers a lesson and initiated a lockout. He thought it would be a "once and for all" solution that would end labor-management clashes, but the Histadrut (general organization of workers—an umbrella organization for all trade unions in Israel) backed the workers' committee. The entire maneuver, initiated by the CEO and his relative, the human resources manager, turned to the worst.

Further complications developed with our largest customer—Alliance Tires. Their much-appreciated CEO, Mr. Teicher, summoned Rogosin representatives for a meeting at his offices in Hadera, declaring that he was not willing to accept frequent supply disruptions, and warning that—unless the outcome of the meeting proves satisfactory—Alliance would immediately cancel all of their orders for the coming year.

Although the CEO kept me in the dark regarding his decisions, following my advice against his idea to implement a lockout, he decided to send me to that meeting with Mr. Teicher, as I was on good terms with him. Alliance was our principal customer, and I went to Hadera with grave concern. I knew that buying from a different supplier would force them to recalibrate all of their machinery (a significant investment of time and money), which could mean that they would not go back to buying from Rogosin.

Teicher expressed his reservations about the CEO's conduct, which he described as irresponsible. He explained that if he had gotten advance warning, he could have prepared a large enough stock of fabric. He said, "We are industrialists, not adventurers, and anyone who decides on a shutdown will have to be responsible for the consequences." A tense silence followed. I told Mr. Teicher, quite emotionally, that I had great respect for him, and I requested to try and figure out what could be done at once. He looked at me and asked what exactly I was offering.

I told him that I was well acquainted with Alliance's specifications and lab result requirements when it came to vulcanization (the press process), and that I was able to obtain large quantities that would meet their needs.

It was a Sunday, and I told him that I was going to Europe the next day in order to obtain fabric that fit Alliance's requirements and ship it to them. I assured him that the product would be identical to what they currently bought from Rogosin. Teicher asked me if I was aware of the magnitude of liability, and, after thinking for a moment, told me to call him on Friday to report on the state of affairs.

The next day I flew to Germany. I first went to Glanzstoff with the purchase order, but they would not accept my terms—that they would let me take over the fabric production process and that I would be the one to calibrate the gauges of the dipping facility. Their refusal meant that I could not be confident in supplying Alliance with the same exact fabric that had identical specifications and quality as the material they were getting from Rogosin.

I did not waste another moment and went that same night to the city of Fulda, where a close friend of mine, Helmut Pilauer, was the purchasing manager at a large factory of high technical capacity. The next morning I arrived at the plant.

I explained my intention to Helmut. In fact, I wanted to stay in Fulda and run one of the shifts so that I could obtain a product according to my requirements. It is not easy for a German factory to accept such an idea. Helmut left the room and came back after about ten minutes with questions, then left again and returned with inquiries about more details, and by the third time I followed him, dodged the receptionist, who tried to stop me but was too slow, and entered a large office where a short aging man stood. He said to me, "I expected you to arrive. Helmut didn't even notice you were walking behind him. . . . Helmut, please leave us."

The Valmiler Factory in Fulda

We sat on opposite sides of a large desk, and he looked me in the eyes and asked, "What is it that you want? Who are you? Which factory do you represent? What is your position there? How come you are fluent in German? Do you have family in Germany? I await your answers to these questions for now." I asked if I could ask for some coffee before I strip. . . . He kept a direct and invasive gaze on me and called out for Elsa, the receptionist, to bring in a lot of strong coffee. He invited me over to a nice more casual seating area and said, "Here we will be more comfortable." I knew that I was all right, at least to begin with.

After coffee and refreshments were served, I spoke for about two hours. I explained that I was born in Berlin and grew up speaking German at home. I told him about my grandfather, a gunnery officer in the German army through seven years, including World War I, who owned seven textile shops in Berlin and immigrated with his family, after the Nazis burned down his shops in 1933, to Palestine, thinking that Nazism was going to be just a passing fad. I told him about Rogosin Enterprise and Alliance Tires, and how I promised Mr. Teicher to supply goods that were a hundred percent identical to the product that Rogosin supplied them, and that my pledge to him was to personally oversee the process. "By Friday," I told him, "I must call Mr. Teicher and confirm that I have been able to secure the supply for his factory as required."

The coffee was already cold, and we didn't even touch it. CEO Herman quietly thought for a while about my terms and said that it would be almost impossible, in his opinion, to find a company that would agree to them.

"It is not about the money," he explained, "It is about letting a man who they have just met take over entire shifts, and we are not talking about one day—this could take three or four months—and even let him calibrate the gouges? That sounds just outrageous! I am over sixty, and I have never, ever heard of such a thing."

He eventually said that he would need four hours to come to a decision and suggested that Helmut Pilauer take me to a good restaurant in the meantime. He said that the prices would not be part of the discussion and, should he agree to my terms, the last word regarding the prices would be his.

Before leaving, I said to him, "No matter what your final decision is, yes or no, it has been my great honor to have met you."

I didn't know what he wanted to check during these four hours, I only knew that unless I was able to strike a deal with the Valmiler factory in Fulda, Rogosin would lose the business of Alliance, and the loss of this customer would mean losing over half of the monthly sales for Rogosin.

The restaurant was charming, warm, and cozy, but as I was too stressed and excited, I only ordered some chicken soup. Helmut shared with me some information about Mr. Herman, who used to be a colonel in the army and had, at that time, headed Valmiler for ten years. I was too tense, but Helmut enjoyed his food and drinks, and four hours later we were back at the plant. Helmut went to his office, and I went to Mr. Herman's. The receptionist kindly offered us fresh coffee and cookies, which she had baked herself. Mr. Herman started by confirming that he was willing to agree to my terms. He listed the prices and explained the terms.

He said that Valmiler would purchase Glanznstoff yarn (the first shipment was already booked and expected within two days) and charge Rogosin for the fabric. He was willing to let me run the shifts and calibrate the gauges. Mr. Herman required a signed declaration from Rogosin to be on his desk by the next day, confirming that Valmiler was not liable for any of the fabrics produced during my shifts and that Rogosin was liable for the relevant materials.

They booked a room for me in a nice hotel and I was expected at the plant first thing in the next morning. That plan was to conduct a meeting with the shift workers and senior staff. Helmut was to update everyone about our arrangement, and I could get a close look at the machinery and equipment. The morning shift supervisor was going to work next to me (and under my supervision) for the first week. And after that, I was going to supervise the evening shifts.

When he was done, Mr. Herman opened a bottle of Cognac and saluted in German. We drank to the occasion, I coughed a bit, and he didn't. Quite spontaneously I hugged Mr. Herman, thanked him and assured him he would not regret his decision. He smiled and said, "One can tell that you are from the Middle-East, a German would never do that." I asked what was it that he found out during the four hours that led him to consent and he told me he had called to confer with Glanzstoff and Dupont, who both replied, once he told them the name of the person he had met, "Yes we know Mr. Knoller very well. He is a man of his word. You can trust him one hundred percent to do whatever he says he will do."

Managing the Production in Fulda

The equipment in the Valmiler plant was almost the same as our equipment in Ashdod, so running it was easy for me. I spent about an hour, before each shift, with the German shift supervisor who tutored me. I calibrated temperature and tension for each and every device, checked end-twist, and it was all working well as if we were back in Ashdod. In the evening I dialed the home number of Mr. Taicher, the CEO of Alliance, and reported back to him. I told him about all that I had achieved so far and that I already had two containers that were ready for shipment, with lab results that complied with the exact same results as the product they usually got from Ashdod.

I promised to send, by the end of that week, the first shipment of six containers on a container ship from Marseille, to arrive five days later in Haifa. Mr. Taicher was thrilled and said, "I value your capability, and you have my everlasting gratitude from now on." I also updated the CEO of Rogosin. He told me there was no progress with the labor union and that their strike was expected to go on for a long time.

The production in Fulda continued smoothly for three months. We carried out a meeting with the plant's CEO. Each shift supervisor provided a weekly report and a schedule for the coming week. The regard for me was so high that sometimes when other shift supervisors had special requirements, they would ask me to present them as mine, assuming that the CEO would not refuse any of my requests.

During that period, Mr. Herman invited me several times to join him in his German Alps cabin, where none of the others, who all feared him, were ever invited. It was an amazing place with a huge library of long-play records. While it snowed heavily outside, we were warm and cozy by the furnace, drinking schnapps and spending long hours in conversation and listening to concerts. He let me into his world and told me about his past. During the Second World War, his rank as head of a labor camp was that of a colonel. One day he told me about a problem he encountered during the war when they could not get resorcinol—the adhesive chemical for sticking rubber and fiber together. I asked him how they solved the problem and he replied that they used blood. I was stupefied. He went on to explain that although it was not as good as resorcinol, it provided the technical solution to this problem. I realized who this person that I was sitting with was, and I also realized that he was oblivious to me being a Jew and an Israeli.

Towards the end of the three-month period, the CEO of Rogosin called to say that the strike was going to end soon and I should get ready to end my stay in Germany. I went to see Mr. Herman and told him that we were about to end our business relations. He seemed surprised and invited me to come with him that weekend to his cabin in the Alps, promising to tell me something.

That weekend he said to me, "Listen, Salomon (he could not pronounce the name Shlomo, so he called me Salomon), I had a meeting this week with the owners of the company in Frankfurt about my nearing retirement, since I am going to be 67 years old soon. I proposed that you, Salomon, should replace me. You are a German who was born in Berlin. I have been following your conduct for the last three months, and you are my candidate."

I needed a few minutes to catch my breath and then I told him, "My dear friend, you forget that I am a Jew, an Israeli, and that I have family—a wife and three daughters—back in Israel. I thank you but in three weeks I am going to return to Israel." He went on to suggest, "Don't be a fool, Salomon," he responded, "you could actually bring your family over here to Germany, drive a Mercedes, earn an excellent salary, and live in a beautiful home here in Fulda—you might wish to reconsider."

During the remaining weeks, we finalized all open orders and accounts. Both the shift workers and the shift supervisors threw several farewell parties on my behalf, and the CEO took me out for an excellent dinner. I told him that he was invited to visit me in Israel, but assumed he would not come.

Upon my return to Israel I found that much had changed. The atmosphere in the plant was grave. The management felt defeated, since the CEO assumed the shutdown would last about two weeks, but it lasted for almost four months. The workers lost a lot of money since the Histadrut organization pledged to help them financially, but eventually provided only half of the promised amount. Thanks to my initiative, the factory did not lose any customers, but still, the losses due to the four-month shutdown were significant.

Mr. Matouk resigned, and once again I put myself up for the position of factory manager. This time, I had more going for me due to my success in maintaining Rogosin's most valuable customer by enabling continuous supply to Alliance, on time, and with the same quality. Shortly after my return, I became the factory manager of Rogosin.

I knew I could achieve the most by concentrating on improving the atmosphere and cooperating with the workers. I consistently met with employees to strengthen this cooperation. The workers' committee resented, to say the least, the fact that I did not conduct all meetings through them. However, at that point, they were much less combative and much more careful and accommodating. We established a soccer team of the factory (I was a stopper) which participated in the workplace-league. A large group of newcomers to Israel, Jews from the Georgian Republic in Western Asia, joined the factory, and I was on very good terms with them.

Both the state of Israel and Rogosin Industries were changing. The Yom Kippur War took place, we were all drafted, and our lives took a wild turn.

The Yom Kippur War

On the eve of the Day of Atonement (Yom Kippur) 1973, we went to the synagogue, then to visit friends, and then back home. It was few months after we had moved to our new home, surrounded by golden sand dunes and facing the blue sea. The ultimate silence of Yom Kippur was disturbed by the ringing of the phone. I was startled, who would dare call at 8:00 a.m. of this day? I picked up the phone, and a recorded official voice instructed me to report at once to the Hatzor Air Force base. I hung up. Edna said, "Calling on the morning of Yom Kippur—such an inappropriate hoax." We went back to sleep but minutes later the phone rang again, and it was Rami, the commander of my military reserve unit, telling me to come to the base immediately. I was in shock. When Edna came up to the table, a coffee pot in her hand, it fell apart, and the coffee spilled all over. We felt as if it were some omen. Edna woke our oldest daughter to care for the younger ones, while she drove me to the base. I was worried that religious fanatics might cast stones, as used to be the case when people showed disrespect for the Day of Atonement by driving.

I soon realized we were not the only car on the road, everyone was on the move. We kissed goodbye and parted, fearing the unknown. I helped with the organizations, equipping everyone with uniforms and arms. A bus took us to the Sinai area. By night, we arrived at the Rephidim base (Bir Gafgafa) in a terrible wind storm. We stopped by a warehouse, where we each got a mattress, and spent the night in a hangar. The next morning everything was very quiet, but by noon we suffered an air strike, which hit the control tower and killed several people.

Following a period of about six months of reserve duty in the Sinai Desert, I was back at work. I was a bit overwhelmed and confused at first, but gradually life was going back to normal. We obtained larger orders and consequently started operating in three shifts. The new workers were quick to fit in, especially the newcomers from Georgia, and the powers divided differently within the worker's committee. CEO Izzy Gilad supported me, and things were going smoothly. A year later Gilad fell sick and died. He was a decisive, organized and honest manager, with the ability to think ahead. In addition, he was well educated and a real gentleman, and I grieved his death.

The American CEO, who had remained uninvolved during the previous years, became more engaged, especially when it came to labor relations. He seemed to have learned nothing at all, from the long strike. The board of directors decided to look at purchasing additional looms and twisting machines, and we found out a Swedish plant that was closing, so I was sent to examine the feasibility of buying their equipment.

The Journey to Sweden

After a long flight and a two-hour drive north of Stockholm, I arrived at the nice hotel booked for me not far from the factory. The factory manager and his wife (she stood six feet seven inches tall, and he was even taller, which made me feel kind of short) were going to take me out to dinner. The freezing weather, as well as the fact that the hotel's fish restaurant was excellent, made us eat there, and after dinner, we sat by the fireplace over a bottle of strong Swedish schnapps, called

Aquavit. We had a long conversation about life in Sweden and Israel, about how the cold weather could be the reason for differences between Israelis and Swedes. To my surprise, the manager's wife lived and worked as a volunteer on an Israeli kibbutz for an extended period and knew much about us. She even indicated that my behavior was not in the typical Israeli manner. Our evening was fabulous; outside the snow accumulated, and inside the Aquavit in the bottle diminished. I feared the arrival of yet another bottle of Aquavit as I thought that could cause me to faint.

The next morning I went to the factory to check the equipment. It was of German origin from the same producer that supplied the machinery used in Rogosin. Operating the machinery would, therefore, pose no problem. The twisting machines were of a different make. Though less efficient, they were easy to work with, being smaller and shorter.

The next step was to discuss prices and draft the terms of the deal. I requested the shipment of the machinery to be done in 40' containers, and we agreed that an engineer from the Swedish factory would spend a month in Ashdod to help us through the assembly and initial operation of the machinery. The agreement was to be approved by both Swedish board of directors and that of Rogosin, and then come into effect within one month.

Upon my return, I submitted a written report, recommending the purchase of the equipment because the equipment could enable a production increase of 25 percent. Also, the equipment was in superb condition, and we could buy it at a very low price.

They sold the equipment because the Swedish environmental authorities instructed them to stop production. Rogosin's CEO, who considered himself a know-it-all, tried to introduce changes to the contract but soon realized that he risked losing this great deal. Eventually, both sides signed, and the deal was realized.

That year, the Institute for Research into Production Efficiency had found Rogosin Industries to be worthy of their Kaplan Prize. The CEO refused to come with me to Jerusalem for the ceremony, so I took Eliahu Cohen, who headed the workers' committee, instead. I was called to the stage at President Katzir's presidential residence, to receive the prize from his hand, and it was an opportunity to tell all the distinguished guests about Rogosin. I presented Eliahu Cohen with the medal, and he has kept it with great pride, on behalf of all the workers of Rogosin enterprise.

Yugoslavian Clients

We had three customers in Yugoslavia. The largest one was a company called Borovo, which owned a large well-established factory about an hour's drive from Belgrade. The others were Zakitz and a company called Record, located next to the Austrian border. They all placed their orders for raw material through a purchasing company in Belgrade. The factories' activity focused on production, and they left the trading part to the Belgrade purchasing office.

The manager of the purchasing company was an elderly Serbian, named Nischewitz, who knew very little about acquisitions. He was given this job due to his history as a renowned partisan and further to being friends with Tito, Yugoslavia's president. And there was more: being head of the secret service for many years, he was known as a fearsome man; he was also a heavy drinker—completely out of focus part of the time, and his favorite pastime was gambling at the Casino. His deputy, Mishkolin, was a bright and most talented man. Mishkolin's wife was the daughter of a well-known communist and veteran partisan hero who used to be a government minister. When the communist party found out that he was not a communist, they demoted him from his ministerial post and thus he became Nischewitz's deputy, which, for the purchasing company, as well as for Nischewitz, was a fortunate turn of events.

I was on good terms with both of them. Whenever I traveled to Dubrovnik, the airport clerk would ask me if I had a visa. I would say "no, I don't," he would ask for four dollars, put two in a box and declare, "this is for Tito," and then put the other two in his pocket without saying anything. That was the way things worked in Yugoslavia. For each one week visit, our customers would prepare schedules, but they were sure to be completely changed upon my arrival so that I would have to extend my stay into three weeks that included excessive drinking of alcohol.

I developed a close friendship with Mishkolin, frequently visited his home and got to know his family. I also got along very well with Nischewitz, and, most important of all, this arrangement secured for Rogosin Enterprise a customer paying five million dollars a year.

Kleber – Fabric for Aircraft Tires

During 1974 the Israeli defense ministry decided to assemble Phantom aircraft's engines onto Mirage planes. This project had some unforeseen consequences; one of them was the higher weight of the engines which caused tires to need replacing after landing the aircraft four or five times. The ministry requested Alliance to produce tires that would withstand at least ten landings, and the feasibility of the entire project depended on their success. Alliance took on the challenge and signed a Knowledge Transfer Agreement with Kleber Tires, which was, at the time, a subsidiary of Michelin.

One of the agreement's requirements was that an Israeli expert would spend six months at the Kleber's plant, in Paris, to study all there was to know about the production process. I was in the middle of military reserve service in Sinai, but Alliance requested that I would be the one to go on behalf of Rogosin. The air force immediately reassigned me, together with four other air force officers, to a crash course that took place in Tel Aviv. We studied French every day from 8:00 a.m. till 7:00 p.m., and after one month I flew over to Paris and studied all there was to know at the Kleber plant. I noted each and every step of their procedure, materials, and solutions. Learning their method of using solutions was a novelty for me—they would mix them in circular tanks, 8 meters in diameter, with four electric propellers. However, they never turned the units on; instead, one of the workers would insert a wooden board through a mixing unit and put it in motion by pacing around the container, as if we were in Biblical times. Further to my expressed amazement, they explained that even at the lowest speed, higher viscosity would form next to the turning propeller, which caused irregular viscosity in the solution. The only way to avoid this was to mix manually.

Back in Israel, we followed the procedures identically to produce the fabrics in the same way as Kleber did, and Alliance used them for the aircraft tires. Tests showed that these tires could even withstand 20 landings. Alliance sent a full report to the French manufacturer, and they were astounded. Three French engineers came to Israel and meticulously examined the entire process at both the Rogosin and Alliance factories. They concluded that the production procedures in Israel and France were identical and could not figure out why the tires made in Israel could withstand twenty landings while those made in France could only withstand ten. Alliance sent several samples to the laboratories of the French air force, and they too could not figure out the source of the difference. A meeting took place at Alliance, in Mr. Teicher's office, attended by the French engineers and myself as the representative of Rogosin. There was a lot of tension in the air as the French suspected the Israelis were concealing information.

I, for one, have figured it out, but I waited for my turn to speak. Mr. Taicher started by saying, "I am the CEO of Alliance and we intend to fully cooperate with you as we wish to learn from your experience and expertise."

After everyone else spoke it was my turn, and I proposed: "Go back to France and install there candid cameras above the tanks." Apparently, the workers at Kleber were tired of walking around the tank and sometimes they would turn the mixer on and go for lunch. The next day the French engineers returned to France and a week later they sent a telegram informing us that the workers of that shift were all laid off and that now all was well. They forwarded their gratitude to me personally.

The End of the Road at Rogosin

Things were going on as usual without any extraordinary events. Whenever my duties took me abroad, my deputy Yossi Segev would take over the management of the tire fabric section, and Avi Sery would replace me in managing the nylon yarn section. Passover was usually when we would sign the coming year's employment contract with the workers' committee. On a meeting with the CEO of Rogosin, a week before the holiday, he informed me that he had hired an assistant director general, to whom I would be subordinate since he was too busy with other activities. My new boss-to-be, was going to be a retired IDF general. The CEO's intention was clear to me. I told him this was a hit below the belt and asked if he wanted me to leave. He promised me that I would receive all that was due to me by law, and sealed his words with: "Happy holiday and goodbye to you." I replied that I would leave upon the arrival of his assistant. I took a long walk along on the seashore and cried for two hours.

During the holiday I was depressed. I obviously needed to find a new venture as soon as possible, and it would probably have to be in a different place. The news traveled fast in Ashdod, and the workers of Rogosin considered sanctions against the management. They came to my home, and I convinced them that it could only cause problems for me. I walked through the factory and parted with each and every person. There were a few tears, and that was it. Sixteen years of work were over.

I had joined Rogosin a young man, fresh out of the kibbutz, as a maintenance mechanic, and left it as a successful factory manager who had acquired vast knowledge through experience from around the world and Israel. There were no other local factories producing tire fabrics or synthetic yarn, but there were many other factories in the textile field, and I was sure there was something for me out there.

Ashdod was our home. Edna and I, as well as our daughters, had many friends, our family was there from the beginning, and we were loved and appreciated. Our new home was on a large lot, the first row to the beach. We had quite a lot to lose should we decide to leave the city.

My parents, who lived in Tel Aviv, used to spend every second weekend with us in Ashdod. They immigrated to Israel in 1934 (when I was four months old) and struggled to make a living in Israel. For many years my father's job involved hard physical labor. My mother did not learn Hebrew and felt detached from Israeli life. They were very proud of the family that Edna and I had established and of our achievements. When they heard of my leaving the factory, they were anxious and feared we would experience hard times. Edna, on the other hand, reacted in a marvelous way. She was confident that we were still young and said, "I trust my husband to find the way." She saw the future through pink glasses.

I waited for the holiday to be over and then I started spreading the word among friends that I was looking for employment. I also approached head hunters and started going to interviews. This period was unpleasant but engaging. Each meeting began with tension: who am I going to see? What would they be offering?

One meeting was with the CEO of Coor Industries. Being a true Yecke, I arrived at the management offices right on time. The receptionist asked me to take a seat and said that the CEO was busy and would see me within a short time. Two other men were sitting there, and they asked me where I was from. They spoke Hebrew with a strong Georgian accent, and when I told them I was from Ashdod, they mentioned the names of their relatives who lived there, and, as it turned out, were Rogosin employees. One of them stepped out to a public phone and then returned and said that his relative told him I was a good man who loved people of Georgian descent. He went on to say that they came to the office first thing in the morning because they were laid off from the Coor factory in Ashkelon "without justice," that the CEO was not ready to see them, that they had raised their voices and threatened to remain there all night. I promised to help them and talk to the CEO about their complaint, they gave me a kiss and left.

Immediately after they left, the receptionist showed me into the CEO's office. He asked her if the two men were still there and added, "What are we going to do about them?" She replied, "Why don't you ask this gentleman? He talked to them and they agreed to leave." The CEO asked me if I was a magician. I told him what their grievance was, that I promised to talk to him on their behalf and was confident he would treat them in a just way.

He offered me a job as the CEO of the Michsaf Company, which produced cutlery. He indicated that he had heard good things about me, and mentioned the Kaplan Prize. It was a good offer, but I was aiming for a larger company, one with thousands of employees, where I would have opportunities for further progress.

A week later I met with Moshe Steigart, the CEO of Kitan, and I immediately knew that I would be glad to work for them, should they choose to hire me. Mr. Steigart explained that Kitan had three factories: Kitan Dimona, Kitan Nazareth, and Kitan Beit She'an. In Dimona, they had about 2,000 employees, in Nazareth 1,700, and in Beit She'an about 1,400. I asked which factory he wanted me to manage, and he told me that he would love to have replaced all three managers, but the highest priority was Beit She'an. The previous manager simply took off and left things in a state of chaos, and the CEO admitted that there were no other candidates willing to take the job. "If you wish to start tomorrow, I would be thrilled. If you can make it there for a year, I would be both thrilled and indebted to you." It was a Monday, and I undertook to start the next week. "Just arrange for a car and someone to take me there," I said. We sealed the agreement with a handshake, and he expressed his fervent hope that I would not regret my decision and wished me great success.

Kitan Factory in Beit She'an

New Beginning in Beit She'an

Mr. Bakal was an assistant director general, managing the production in Kitan, and he was the one who took me from Tel Aviv to Beit She'an. He had come to Israel from Romania five years earlier and was ten years older than me. During the three-hour ride, I felt we were becoming friends. He told me about the human element in the factory, about the violence that had become widespread there, and about four managers who, one after the other, had not lasted more than four months.

According to Bakal, gangs controlled the plant, and in that sense, the task that I took upon myself was risky, even regarding my own physical safety. He was certain that success could open many doors for me in the future.

The gate opened, and I saw a large U-shaped building surrounding an open courtyard. A large group of people stood there, and it almost looked like a demonstration. To be frank, it felt a bit intimidating.

A robust man stepped forward and approached me introducing himself as David, head of the workers' committee. I shook his hand very firmly, and it surprised him. I looked him in the eyes and presented myself: "My name is Shlomo, I am your new manager." He returned my gaze and looked back into my eyes. Despite a remote sense of awkwardness, I had a feeling that David and I were going to be able to work together.

Bakal and I went into the management building where the offices of the manager, secretary, human resource manager, and production engineer, were located. The secretary, a very young woman of eighteen, presented herself: "My name is Ester, I am your secretary at your service. I cooked for you a dish of okra, do you like okra?" I replied, "Okra is not part of the job description. What I don't like is a secretary cooking for the factory manager. From now on there should be no cooking—there is a dining room in the factory, and everyone eats there."

The manager's office was a spacious room, but its walls were scribbled, and it was utterly dirty. I asked for the maintenance manager and introduced myself. Before I had a chance to say anything he said, "We know who you are and we already found out how long you are going to stay here." I told him it was none of his business and requested that he immediately arrange for two people to paint the walls and then clean the floors and windows. I told him the office was to be sparkling clean by the next morning. He looked at me in amazement and asked, "All this by tomorrow? Most unlikely!" I told him it is up to me to determine what is likely, and that this was what I expected of him. On his way out I heard him say, "This manager is not normal."

Bakal and I toured the plant, starting at the large 30,000 spindles textile mill. I was informed that the production yield was 4 to 5 tons of yarn per day. I asked Bakal if it was low and he replied that it was a very low yield. Further to my next question as to the reasons he replied, "Lack of control over what was going on here." We went on to look at the dyeing facility, where part of the equipment was out of order, and at the printing facility some of the machinery was not operating because the color kitchen was unable to supply the printing facility with paint. I started to understand what lack of control meant.

At the end of the day, I took Bakal back to Tel Aviv, and when he asked me for my opinion I took some time to reply and then said that I thought the situation was grim, but that I believed Beit She'an could be turned into a profitable factory. It was not going to be done in one day. I needed to learn what was going wrong, prepare a plan, form a budget, and introduce discipline into the work culture. I intended to draw a preliminary plan within three months. Bakal said that according to what he saw that day he was confident that assigning me to manage the factory was a good decision, promised to report to the CEO and to support me, and told me that he believed I would make a success of it.

I called Edna in Ashdod, told her about the first day and asked her to come for several days to Beit She'an to help me set up the apartment I had received. At night I drove to Yokne'am for the night at Edna's parents' house. I spent only a short time with them before falling asleep.

The following morning I left Yokne'am at 6:00 and arrived in Beit She'an at 7:00. My office had been painted over and cleaned during the night. Though not perfect, it was reasonable. At 8:00 a.m., the maintenance manager arrived, looked at the result, and asked if I was content. I told him that the workers who did the job were OK but that I would have expected him to be the first person arriving, to make sure everything was satisfactory. He murmured something that sounded like "A tough character" and left. I made my point: one must work hard to satisfy the demands of this annoying manager....

The secretary arrived at 9:00 a.m. When she entered, she couldn't believe the room was the same one she remembered from the day before. I told her she was expected to come to work at 8:00 a.m., and her reply was, "And what if I don't?" I said, "In that case, I would reassign you to work at the mill." She grabbed her purse and said, I am going to complain to the workers' committee. Within a short time the security person—who was in fact supposed to have been my bodyguard—came to my office and started yelling at me and threatening. He was still swearing and describing what he was going to do to me, as he was leaving. I called Steigart, the CEO, to tell him what was going on, and he assured me that I had his full support. I knew that the power struggle that would determine who controlled the factory, had begun.

Power Struggle

During the first three months, the parties checked each other out. I was confident that a full blown clash was inevitable within a short time and assumed that the longer it took to happen, I would be better prepared for it. In the meantime production in the textile mill was growing. We had already reached a daily yield of 9 tons of yarn. Every day at 4 p.m. I called a department managers' meeting to discuss the daily yield and any hurdles. I started learning and mapping coalitions and rivalries amongst people, attended several bar mitzvah and wedding celebrations, and formed alliances with some workers. The employees could be classified as follows: 500 from Beit She'an, 300 Arab workers from Umm al-Fahm, 200 Druze people from Mrar, and several hundreds of people from other places. The people of Beit She'an dominated the workers' committee, and even they were divided into groups among them.

I resided in Beit She'an, staying home with my family only on Tuesday nights and during the short weekends from Friday noon to Sunday early morning.

It was hard for me and my family, and we reluctantly decided to sell our Ashdod home and move north by the end of the school year. We rented a place in Tiv'on, and began building a home in Yokne'am. It was not an easy decision. I could have found an executive job in the vicinity of Ashdod, one that might be less invigorating and autonomous, but that would have let us avoid the jolts and complications to our family life.

Edna and I spent many sleepless nights in hesitations and thought. In the long run, we saw many advantages of building a home in the fields of Yokne'am, and, following much contemplation, we decided to move north. I foresaw advancement prospects in Kitan, expected to seize the opportunity it offered me and make a success of it. We wanted to have a large lovely house, plant a fruit orchard, bring up our girls within the agricultural moshava culture, and never regret our choice. In Beit She'an, things were also going well. First of all, the secretary left and Tamar took her place. Tamar was a lovely woman who was married to Yechezkel, one of the factory's drivers. She was well liked in the factory, especially among the group of Iraq-descendant employees. I found an esteemed figure to be on my side and help me.,

Every day at the factory was an unexpected adventure. Things did not completely quieten down, but there was some slow improvement. One day, walking around the factory, I noticed a gathering in the yard. The security guard, surrounded by some 300 people was making loud remarks about the factory manager being a security risk and stating that the workers should have him fired. When he saw me coming, he started swearing at me. I approached and the other people moved back. I came so close to him that my face was almost touching his, and said in a loud voice: "Show me you are a man and come with me." He muttered something but the workers around him shouted: "Armond, be a man, go with him." I walked to my car, which was not far from there, opened the door and said, "Come in." He was reluctant, but the other workers were rooting and shouting, "Go with him,

Armond!" So he got in and we drove off. As soon as we were on our way, he asked, "Where to?" in a scared voice. He then went on to say, "I did not really mean it like that, it was a joke, I am your friend, don't worry, I will be there for you and help with all that you need. . . ."

I took him to a national park called Sakhne. When he got out of the car I suddenly punched him in the stomach and he fell to the ground. I kicked him, smeared his face in mud and left him there. Back at the factory some workers asked me where he was and I said, "He is bathing at the Sahne Park, go get him."

Beit She'an was a small town and the story spread in no time. After a few days, he phoned me and asked for a meeting. We met in a café in a town nearby, and when I arrived, on time, he was already there. He started crying and told me that he was a drug addict and sometimes, when under the influence, he had no control over his behavior. He said that he loved me and was willing to die for me and it was only the drugs that made him behave that way. I asked what he proposed, and he told me that he had become the laughing stock of Beit She'an, promised never to show his face at the factory and requested his severance pay. I shook his hand, arranged for his due payments and he kept his word. I was held in high esteem by the factory workers, following this episode.

A week later, Mr. Steigart came for a visit with the CEO of Clal Industries, Mr. Zvi Tsur. General Tsur's nickname was Tchera, and before Clal he was the IDF's Chief of Staff, served for seven years as an adviser to the Minister of Defense, Moshe Dayan, and had several managing positions in mega companies.

Our paths crossed many times from then on. I considered him a friend and found him to be an extraordinary person. We walked through the clean production facilities and I showed them that all was working properly.

Back at the office, Zvi Tsur told me that the day before he had met a mutual friend—Yisrael Ben-Yehuda. Tsur confessed that when Ben-Yehuda said that the new Beit She'an factory manager claimed to be able to produce 11 tons of yarn per day at the textile mill, while only 4 tons a day were produced under the previous manager, he thought it was just boasting. Ben Yehuda assured him though, that it was not only an intention but already an achievement. Tsur shook my hand and said, "I know now that Yisrael was right and I admire what you have done." He looked at Steigart and said, "If only we had two more managers of the same caliber, our company would be on the right track."

Fun Activities for Employee's Children

During one meeting I proposed a boat trip on the Sea of Galilee for all of the worker's children, to celebrate the Chanukah holiday. Some of the comments were: "They would be incontrollable," "We can't take the responsibility, and they might fall overboard," "They don't deserve such a treat."

Since a factory is not a democracy, I decided to make my proposal work. Some 800 Jewish, Arab, and Druze kids gathered in the factory dining room, each received a glass of chocolate milk and pastry. We asked them to behave and assigned a grownup to each boat. The trip was a great success, the children's behavior was impeccable, and both parents and children were very pleased.

There was significant improvement at the factory, but we still faced many problems, among them an excess of workers and the fact that the weaving department was outdated with looms that were slow and small. Since Kitan Enterprise had a new weaving department in Dimona that had faster looms and was highly professional, I thought it redundant to operate both units. I submitted a report to Mr. Steigart, and the Kitan board concluded that my suggestion could save large sums of money. As it was evident that such a move would not go through peacefully, I was requested to prepare for it and determine the timetable.

Meeting with David Levi

Several political figures in Beit She'an were involved in all that was going on in the factory, and the most prominent one was David Levi. Born in Morocco, and initially a blue-collar worker and union activist, he was a government minister, and an influential and wise man who did his best to represent the less powerful echelons of society.

Kitan meant a lot to him and four family members of his, including a brother and a brother-in-law, were members of the factory workers' committee. I went to see him one evening on the weekend. We sat on his porch, and he was interested to hear how I was doing and what the situation in the factory was. I told him about the security guard incident, which he was aware of, and went on, quite openly, to explain that the factory was losing money and has an oversized workforce. I talked of some unacceptable norms such as workers who parked their private cars within the premises of the plant or took fabric at will in addition to the twice-a-year bonus of a fabric package given to each worker (which was, in fact, simply theft) that were widespread in Kitan Beit She'an. I explained that, unless changes were made, Clal Industries, who owned Kitan, would stop trying and close the factory, which sustained hundreds of families. I could tell that nothing I said was news to him, and he agreed to support steps to correct that situation, as long as they were fair and square. I went on to meet with the mayor and the town's chief rabbi and had a feeling that I had a long way to go, but I was on the right track.

Since keeping the factory going with existing losses and norms was not an option, Steigart and I decided the weaving department had to be shut down, and unacceptable standards stopped. We expected to meet with strong opposition, and I told Steigart that the options were either to deal with a long-term strike, or close the factory down. He asked me to implement the changes and said he was willing to support me in any way I needed.

I met the workers' committee at my office, and told them that the board of Clal decided to shut down the weaving department. There was a long shocked silence, followed by everyone shouting at once. One of them even picked up his chair and smashed the window. The head of the committee hollered, "No way, under no circumstances." All of the workers gathered in the yard and then most of them left the place. Clal hired a security company that employed guards that were not living in Beit She'an to secure the premises. The maintenance manager and I turned off the electricity connection.

I reported back to Mr. Steigart and told him that I had asked the junior management not to show up the next day, but that I would be there. The Druze and Arab workers did not come to work the next day, but 200 residents of Beit She'an jumped the fence, shouted and rioted, and even threatened to kill me. Some ten journalists arrived, took pictures, spoke with the workers' committee and with me, and after several hours it was over.

I thought that they might arrange to take everyone in buses to demonstrate in front of the Tel Aviv Clal headquarters, so I asked

Steigart to come to Beit She'an. He arrived the next day, but the workers did not come to meet with him.

The Breakthrough

A month after the strike started, I got a phone call from David Edry, who headed the workers' committee and was David Levi's brother-in-law, asking for a one-on-one meeting away from Beit She'an. We met at a café in Tivon. He was a wise young man, a natural leader appreciated by the workers. He asked me what was going to happen and I said it was up to the workers. I emphasized that rioting and violence could not solve the problem, that a company like Clal could not be forced into maintaining a factory that was in a loss, and that I thought we both knew that things were not going to go back to how they used to be. I asked if he wanted to go back to work and he said, "Yes, and I have a feeling it should be done soon or else there would be no workplace to go back to." Edry requested a meeting between management and the workers' committee at David Levi's office, in the Jerusalem government complex.

Steigart and I arrived on time, and upon their arrival (half an hour late), Minister David Levi started by describing the history of the factory in Beit She'an. He then indicated that the livelihood of hundreds of families depended on Kitan, being the employer of some 800 residents. He complimented me by saying that I was the first manager to be a real professional, and a man who set a personal example and had demands and requirements that caused to lead the factory forward.

CEO Steigart agreed and further added that the factory employed 1,400 workers, but only 800 or even less were required. Violence and threats, let alone theft, he said, hindered the performance of the factory. He assured the workers that the owners would be willing to reopen the plant only if they could run it as an effective and efficient factory that could produce good quality products at costs that allowed for profitability. He concluded by saying, "If you do not agree to our terms, there will be no Kitan factory in Beit She'an."

That immediately caused an outburst. One committee member stood up and shouted, "We shall not surrender to the Ashkenazi's (Jews of European descent). You want to fight us? We'll fight back! Neither you nor Shlomo Knoller, have control over the factory. Only the workers' committees are going to call the shots, as they know what is best for Beit She'an." One of them called out to David Levi: "How come you go along with them? Have you forgotten your origins?" David Levi asked us to leave the room and come back after about three hours.

We went out to grab a bite and discussed the situation. I told Steigart that I thought he should not back off and that I believed David Levi could solve this with the workers. He said that were it not for me, he would have by then closed the factory already.

When we returned, only half of the committee members were still there. David Levi said that, having examined the main problems, they agreed to the terms in general and that those who would not be willing to accept should be allowed to leave and receive due severance payments. He requested a detailed plan for future procedures, arranged to meet with the committee on Thursday, and asked that I meet with David Edry on Friday. The factory was to reopen in the coming week. Steigart agreed and said he would come for the reopening after the weekend. The headlines in all national newspapers reported a breakthrough in negotiations and the chance for the factory to start working again.

On Friday I had a meeting with Edri, and we worked out the details. We set up criteria that took into account parameters such as workers' seniority, age, family status, and the number of children. Creating such a list was a harsh and painful process, but there was no doubt in our minds that it was better than the sudden and abrupt source of income loss for all of the workers.

Within three months, the factory recuperated and productivity went up significantly. Since Kitan compensated anyone who willingly resigned, many took advantage of this option, which lessened the impact of the mass layoffs. We took steps to create social activities and initiated a soccer team that eventually rose to second place in the northern league. Jewish, Druze, and Arab workers played together, and the team was imperative in the social integration among employees. We also initiated activities that we called "Circle of Companions." Participants got together twice a month after working hours. Once a month we would go to Tiberias for a bathe at the hot springs, and dinner, singing on our way back to Beit She'an; and once a month we would bring some interesting activities to the plant. The atmosphere at Kitan Beit She'an was productive and pleasant, and it was no longer on the brink of closing down.

One day my office door opened, and I was surprised to see Arik Sharon, a celebrated general due to his part in the Yom Kippur War, at the entrance. He was surprised, too, and asked, "Are you not the guy from my Mom's tea party in Kfar Malal?"

"Well," I said to him, "I think it was the cake that took center stage there, not the tea." I invited him in, offered tea, and apologized for the lack of cake. Arik told me that he had established a new political party, called Shlomzion, and that they intended to put themselves up for the next Knesset elections. He wanted me to take him to the plant's dining room so that he could deliver his speech and try to recruit voters.

Such a move could have been problematic for me, as Clal Industries that owned Kitan was historically established by the socialist Histadrut trade union and was managed by people from the left side of the political map. I refrained from going with him and asked the human resources manager to take him instead. Everyone rose to welcome him with "Arik King of Israel" calls. He spoke with great enthusiasm and concluded by saying, "You must vote for Shlomzion. I spoke with your manager and offered him the fourth place in my party. He is going to be a Knesset Member." Of course, there was no truth in this declaration, and even if he had offered this to me, I would not have agreed. Come election day, almost all of the residents of Beit She'an voted for the Likud party....

Investing in the Factory

I presented Kitan with a development plan for the factory, proposing to invest in cutting-edge high-velocity textile printing machinery. After thorough research, I proposed to purchase a 12-color rotary machine from the Swiss Buser company. I visited Buser, and a couple of mechanics were sent there to learn the maintenance procedures. It was a very substantial investment that required workers to develop technical abilities and could place Kitan in another league altogether within the industry.

An episode from my first days in Kitan Beit She'an can best illustrate the extent to which the company had changed and developed. One morning I came to my office and found a dead cat on my desk, head and body apart, and in the gap a black lettered note: "To the attention of factory manager. Leave Beit She'an instantly, or else this is your end!" I was in a shock and wanted to resign at once. Beit She'an's Chief Rabbi shortly came and took me out for coffee. He asked me not to leave, argued that if I threw in the towel, I might never forgive myself, and assured me that better days would come. About a year later I found out who were the perpetrators and called them into my office and fired them. The horrible sight, I told them, would always stay in my mind. They asked for my forgiveness, but I told them to ask the Lord for forgiveness.

Three years later, we were surprised to find out that Kitan's management decided to invest yet another large sum in the Beit She'an factory. We mostly needed to improve the color kitchen. I could have sent someone to Switzerland to study the technology, but I preferred to bring in a professional that would introduce not only their knowledge but also the European work culture.

I decided to go at it by advertising in German industry magazines a call for a professional that would be willing to come to Israel and work there for a period of at least one year as head of the color kitchen. Eight people applied. I flew over for three days to meet three of them in Frankfurt, spent a day with each candidate and chose the third. He was in his fifties, highly experienced, and wanted time away from Germany due to a recent painful divorce. We set him up in a kibbutz nearby, arranged for Hebrew lessons twice a week, so that he could better communicate, and assigned two workers, one of them a Yiddish speaker, to accompany him. It was a great success, both professionally and socially. He had many friends among the workers and became involved in soccer as well, and his influence on the work culture was vast. I used to spend the day with him once a month and I learned from him a lot about his profession.

Kitan Beit She'an was becoming profitable. I developed a plan for the production of different kinds of blended yarn, mainly polyester and cotton. I went to Germany to find a supplier, sent the maintenance manager to get trained, and in three months Kitan was able to offer a variety of cotton-polyester blends.

CEO Mr. Steigart invited me one day to a meeting in Tel Aviv. He took me to a lovely restaurant by the sea and ordered for us two glasses of whiskey. I asked what were we celebrating and he said, "Wish me luck, I am leaving Kitan." It was quite shocking for me, as the company was doing well, all of its factories were working at full capacity, there were many orders and Kitan was profitable. Steigart said that he believed a successful manager should leave when things have been going well for several years and not when the company is in bad shape. He said, "I am a big boy and I know what I'm doing," and explained that he didn't want me to hear the news through hearsay and wanted to tell me in person.

Steigart assumed that Nehemia Cain, who was to take his place, was acquainted with me. When listing the names of factory managers in Kitan, Steigart told me, Cain said, "Shlomo Knoller is the best manager to join Kitan, following four managers who ran away. He has been managing Kitan Beit She'an for the last five years and has turned it from a failing factory into a successful enterprise." I told Steigart that I had never met him and all I had heard about him was that he was not one to be generous with compliments and that whenever he made mistakes, people told him, "Under Knoller this would never happen." So he probably couldn't even bear to hear my name.

At the end of our meeting, I told Steigart how much I enjoyed working with him and expressed my deep appreciation for his conduct. "Any success we have been able to achieve," I said to him, "is due to the support that you provided." We shook hands, and it was the end of an era.

Working with Nehemia Cain

The new CEO came for a visit in Beit She'an and we visited each of the departments. We then went back to my office, and it was clear that we were assessing each other like two wrestlers. He was clearly aware that I must have had inquired about him through my connections at Rogosin and he told me all about his time there and how difficult it was to work with the CEO. He mentioned that everyone there praised my management of Rogosin, and expressed his confidence that we would get along well together. I said as little as possible, and after four hours he went on to the next factory. I knew that since Steitgart was not longer in Kitan, I had to conduct myself with great caution.

On the home front, we were renting in Tiv'on, Michal attended high school in Kiryat Bialik, Ruth went to school in Tivon, and Tamar in Kfar Yehoshua. We were happy and content, and we thoroughly enjoyed living in the beautiful home with a lovely garden in Tiv'on.

Nehemia Cain visited Beit She'an at least once a month, and I arranged for a meeting with the heads of all the departments. He did his best to be liked and used to tell jokes while carefully checking who was not laughing. When someone didn't laugh, he would make sure to explain the joke to them. Sometimes he would bring Zvi Tsur, who was his immediate superior, along. He ensured that he would be the one to guide Zvi Tsur through the different departments.

The color kitchen was the most striking department. The workers, all in white robes, were bustling, and the place looked as clean and tidy as a Hilton kitchen. Zvi Tsur wanted to talk with the German maister and again, Nehemia Cain was eager to be the one to interpret, but the German could not understand him, so they turned to me to do the translation. The maister explained to Tsur that he had never expected to ever work in Israel until he responded to a classified ad. A week later he got a call from Mr. Knoller, whom he thought was a German, maybe from Berlin. He told Tsur that he was extremely happy working in Beit She'an and planned to stay for a long time. While we were walking back to my office, Zvi Tsur said to Nehemia, "This is the kind of managers we need for Kitan. I have never seen the Beit She'an factory in such good condition as during this visit today." Before leaving, he shook my hand and said, "Shlomo, it was a pleasure. Well done!"

The visits did not always have such pleasant tones. A month later, the printing department workers demanded a raise in salary. According to the agreement, salary discussions took place only once a year, so I refused to negotiate with them. Nehemia Cain heard about it and arrived without advance notice. He came to my office, had a cup of coffee with me and disappeared. Tamar, my secretary, told me that the CEO called her home number the evening before. He made some small talk, and then asked her about what was going on in the printing department. She told him to ask me, so he ended the call wishing her a good night.

This meant we were waging our first battle. I looked for him in the printing department, but he was nowhere to be seen, except the workers pointed towards the color kitchen. When I opened the door, I saw him sitting and talking to the printing manager and his deputy and heard the words, "Nehemia, we deserve more." They were startled, and my first words were, "Nehemia Cain, this doesn't look good." I asked the workers to get back to work at once and asked Nahemia to join me at my office. I closed the door behind me and then said: "I suggest that you come to a decision whether you want us to continue to work together. Don't do things behind my back, it appears dishonorable. Should we go down that path, I will be walking away from here without looking back." There was a silence, and I know that Nehemia Cain was calculating in his head. As long as Beit She'an was doing well, my staying was in his best interest, and also, he wouldn't want Zvi Tsur to know that he had a conflict with me.

There was never a dull moment in Beit She'an. Families of the young Arab women from Umm al-Fahm found out that during the night shifts, they would talk to the young Druze men from the village of Mrar. They refused to allow them to work the evening and night shifts. Such a situation could have caused the mill to shut down. I went to see the mayor of Umm al-Fahm, along with the parents, at the city hall. Several parents said that the money the young women earned was significant, but that their family's honor was even more important. I offered a creative solution: Kitan would hire twelve older women whose job would be to chaperone the young women. They were astonished, and after I had confirmed that the older women would be paid a full salary, we came to a mutual agreement. All parties were eventually content, perhaps except for the young men from Mrar, but the most important thing for me was that the mill could operate at full capacity with three shifts.

Nehemia Cain was worried about the situation in the mill as we had large orders that needed to be filled out, and when I informed him about the solution, he was extremely glad about it. The next time he visited we even went out for lunch in Ma'ayan Harod, where I used to dine with Steigart once a month.

A Surprising Proposition

Looking back at over five years of my work in Beit She'an, the transformation in the factory seemed unbelievable. Production was running smoothly, the mill produced 11-12 tons of yarn per day (about 10 tons of cotton yarn, and the rest, cotton-polyester blends). The production in the mill and in other departments, including the printing and dyeing facilities and flannel production line, reached its maximum capacity operating five days a week in three shifts. We went on to dye yarn in addition to fabric. The atmosphere and social changes were fantastic too. Our soccer team (where my position as a defender was secured further to my abilities only) had reached the top of the workplace league in northern Israel.

Our Circle of Companions was a means for benefitting those who deserved it. It became so desirable that some workers, who were not included, even offered to pay their way into the circle.

One day, the CEO called to let me know he was coming the next day. He closed my office door behind him and told me in confidence that Razi Ben-Porat, Kitan's deputy general manager for fashion and clothing, was suddenly leaving. I later found out that when both of them were on their way to the United States, Cain criticized Ben-Porat and put him down throughout the entire flight. Ben-Porat took it to heart, resigned, and decided not to come back to Israel.

The fashion branch operated as an independent company within Kitan. The fashion market was most challenging and complicated and its turnover was massive. Nehemia Cain offered me this position, with the prospect of becoming a deputy general manager in Kitan after one year—if I was successful. The question of my success (or failure) was to be determined by Cain himself. He indicated that Zvi Tsur was extremely appreciative of my achievements in Beit She'an, but further emphasized that the final decision was going to be up to him.

When he was through, I offered him coffee, thanked him for the trust he put in me, and asked to send him my reply by fax, the next morning. Nehemia was a bit surprised and murmured, "I am sure you are aware of the fact that there are many other eager candidates for this job." I thanked him again and expressed my confidence in my ability to perform successfully, should I decide to take on this job, and repeated that I needed some time to think it over and make up my mind.

After Nehemia Cain had left, I told Tamar, my secretary, that I was going out and would return in the afternoon. She asked if I needed anything and I said, "No, nothing." She knew me well and could see that I was stirred up. I went to the Sahne National Park. It was a sunny winter day, the sun was pleasantly warm, and I sat down to analyze the offer I was given, which had come as a total surprise. It was a sharp diversion from my professional direction; a transition that would lead me away from managing a factory to the areas of sales, advertising, and finance, to managing some twenty stores and traveling abroad, and it meant that I would not always be able to make my own decisions. I sat there until it was getting dark and then returned to the office to prepare my reply.

I started by thanking Nehemia Cain wholeheartedly for his offer. I went on to state that I was willing to take on this job, on the condition that immediately upon my arrival in Kitan's headquarters at Hadar Yosef, from day one, I would have the position of deputy general manager, including full authority, salary, and benefits—the same as held by my predecessor.

I guessed that this precondition would infuriate Nehemia Cain, but assumed he had no other candidate and could not find an available one within a short time. In the fashion industry, time is crucial, and a vacuum is not an option as you must come up with a new collection on time, or else you miss an entire year.

Furthermore, I was sure Nehemia Cain had already told Zvi Tsur that he was offering this job to me, and refusing me would put him in an awkward position, having to specify the reasons. I placed a bet with a calculated risk.

Tamar, who waited for me back at the office, printed my reply and faxed it over to Nehemia Cain that evening. The next morning, during my morning tour through the factory, Tamar caught up with me in the printing department and told me Nehemia Cain had already called twice, sounding extremely nervous, and that he wanted me to immediately call him back. I rang him, and he shot at me like a cannonball: "You think you're a smart guy? You're a Schmuck!" and hung up, slamming the phone down.

In fact, I actually feared worse consequences, as I knew Nehemia Cain was smart and ambitious. If he had another candidate he would think to himself, "I gave that scoundrel a chance and he didn't take it? Well, that is his problem, and I did my best." I assumed that if he had no other candidate, he would work out the same considerations as me, swallow his ego and go along with my demands. Three days later he called and said that he had accepted my terms, that I would receive an official fax within an hour, and he ended the call by saying, "You are still both a scoundrel and a shmuck!"

I know that my bet was well placed, and I triumphed. However, I was aware of the risk that victory would come at a cost. Working with Nehemia Cain, one could never have a weak spot. You had always to be successful in order for him to boast that it was him who brought on that success, but if you failed you were doomed. Struggles with him were better to be channeled towards the way things were done, and if you were successful, he was sure to join the same road. There had been some opposition in Kitan to my nomination, but Nehemia Cain stood up for me, including an incident where one of the high ranking executives tried to claim for himself my predecessor's office space, which was in a highly regarded location, and Nehemia Cain himself threw him out of there.

I was replaced in Beit She'an by Yossi Segev, who used to be my deputy at Rogosin. Nehemia Cain did not confide in me, and Yossi himself did not talk to me, before accepting this job. I felt that a hardcore workplace like the Beit She'an factory was not a suitable place for Segev's character. We only had one week of overlapping integration period before I moved on to my new job at Hadar Yosef in Tel Aviv.

On my first workday as Kitan's fashion manager, Nehemia Cain came to my room and said, "I will not be in your way, you go ahead and do what you want to. I just wanted to let you know that a week ago I fired the head designer of Kitan and have made a public announcement to that effect." He made it clear that he would not agree, under any circumstances to rehire her. At the time I had little knowledge as to who was that designer, what were the roles of a head designer, what were the alternatives, significance, and consequences. The newspapers published items about my nomination; one headline read, "Kitan went crazy and placed a cowboy at the head of their fashion department." They described me as a farmer from Yokne'am Village, working in the company headquarters on workdays and farming the land on the weekends.

Entering The Fashion World

Kitan Company, Tel Aviv

Every morning I would set out for a very early drive to Tel Aviv, and by at 7:30 a.m. I was already seated at my desk, reading the mail and preparing my daily schedule. My Yecke secretary, Miriam, would arrive at 8:00 a.m. sharp and serve me a cup of coffee. As the building was waking up, I would visit the modeling hall and sewing workshop. I was in charge of about twenty workers in the modeling hall, and over twenty shops located throughout Israel. My soundtrack changed from the noise of heavy machinery to the sound of people in the hallways of the large building where about 200 people worked hard to secure employment for about 3,500 industry workers, not necessarily an easy job, and a heavy responsibility.

During the first week, I studied the problems, attempting to figure out the orders of importance and priorities. The first crisis I encountered started with a phone call in English from a lady with a thick German accent. It was Mrs. Achten, from Hertie, in Germany, asking for Mr. Ben Porat. I replied in German and told her I was Ben Porat's successor, as he no longer worked for Kitan, and that it was my first day on the job. She was calling to inform that Hertie had received a defective shipment of skirts, which they were shipping back to Israel. I offered a substantial discount instead, but she immediately replied, "I assume you are a German and in that case, you must know that Hertie does not sell second rate goods. Besides, your container is already back at the port, scheduled to leave tonight. I am sorry, and I wish you all the best in the future."

I checked the skirts and saw the defect, so I called an emergency meeting and invited managers of the sewing workshop and the modeling hall as well. All of the participants were experienced workers with a record of over ten years in Kitan. I described the situation and asked them to think what course of action they would have chosen in the face of such negligent sawing and lack of quality control prior to packing and shipping.

The sales manager, who was deputy to Ben Porat, proposed to advertise a special offer under the slogan: "Women of Israel, we have left behind a small quantity of a line exported to Germany. Get European fashion at a discount." He estimated we could sell the entire quantity, and even make a profit. I asked if there were other opinions and everyone thought this was the best solution. I reported to Nehemia Cain. "Tomorrow morning I am in Dimona," he said, "and heads will roll."

Fashion Designer

For almost a month I hectically searched for a new fashion designer. The marketing of fashion and clothing is not at all possible without a leading and experienced designer who can create, twice a year, a collection encompassing hundreds of items. Kitan supplied its goods to over 20 company stores and to dozens of traders. We urgently needed a prominent and experienced designer, or else Kitan stood to suffer great losses. I could see it coming. My investigation as to why Kitan's designer was fired revealed that Nehemia Cain ended her employment for reasons that had nothing to do with her professional performance. She was hard working and skilled, excelled at her job, and had a significant role in Kitan's success.

I decided, despite Nehemia Cain's warnings, to try and win her back. I called Mrs. Shafir, introduced myself and asked for a meeting. She hung up on me right after saying, "Are you the cowboy Kitan brought in to head the fashion department? We have nothing to talk about!" I drove to Ramat Aviv, went up to her sixth-floor apartment and rang the doorbell. I could see that someone was looking through the peephole, and when the door opened, a gorgeous young lady asked, "And with whom do I have the honor?" I replied, "I am the cowboy and I would love a cup of coffee." We sat at the kitchen table, and she got all of her anger and frustration off her chest. I gave her my word of honor that she would have no contact whatsoever with Nehemia Cain, only with me.

Within a short time Nehemia Cain found out what I had done and barged into my office with raging fury. After about five minutes of screaming, Miriam brought him a glass of water. He stopped yelling but was not at all content. We agreed to meet at a café the next day, and I explained to him in detail why we had no other options. Nehemia Cain was a smart man, so he knew I was right. I finally said to him, "If you insist, I will let her go but I too will leave Kitan." He got up to leave, muttering, "Pay for the coffee."

I worked with Miri Shafir, in full coordination, for five years and never regretted this move for even one moment.

Fashion is a fascinating industry. A fortune can be made instantly, and at the same time large sums can be lost within a short time. It is highly recommended not to deal with it without proper background and knowledge. In Israel, where the market is tiny, exporting is essential, and this makes things even more complicated.

On January 1972, at the Hilton Amsterdam, Kitan participated in an Israeli show, showcasing some thirty Israeli fashion companies.

It opened with a large fashion show for all of the companies, and on the third night, Miri Shafir choreographed an astonishing theatrical and musical show for Kitan with 16 models. It was almost as elaborate as a musical. The place was packed with spectators and buyers, who were the main target audience. During the show, I got word that Mrs. Achten was going to be there the next day. I asked the Israeli representative of Hertie to bring Mrs. Achten to Kitan's rooms first. He was willing to do that on several conditions; the one that bothered me the most was that I would move aside and let him guide her, but I agreed. The next day he brought her over and during her tour, despite my promise, I came over and asked Mr. Achten if she remembered me. I reminded her that she sent back to Israel a full container of skirts on my first day on the job. She said, "I do remember and I wished to make your acquaintance." I assured her that I would be more than happy and added, "Same as you had the guts to send that shipment back, I hope you have the guts to make a purchase now." She invited me over to Hertie's headquarters in Frankfurt with the new collection and said, "I hope we can continue where we left off." I gave her a kiss on the cheek, and she went on her way. Hertie's representative almost fainted. Not only did I break my promise to be silent while he spoke, but I also got an invitation to visit Hertie in Frankfurt, whereas he was not invited.

The Sales to Hertie

One week after the show was over, I went to Frankfurt with the collection to show it to Mrs. Achten, who was the purchasing manager of Hertie. She reined over about three hundred huge stores in Germany and all over Europe. The position of purchasing manager was that of the power behind the throne. Purchasing managers were a significant component in the success of a company. They held the reins when it came to procurement decisions, what and how much to buy, and could make or break their suppliers. They were aware of all this and behaved accordingly.

I arrived at Hertie's headquarters, a 25-story large building, and entered the spacious and lavish lobby. After registering at the reception, I suddenly spotted Nehemia Cain there. He asked me what time our meeting was scheduled for, and I explained to him that they would call us up when they were ready for us. He went over to the reception manager and asserted: "I am the CEO of the Kitan Company and I am also a General in the IDF. Please let Mrs. Achten know that I am booked on a flight back to Israel this evening, and therefore request that she will see us as soon as possible."

After about half an hour, Nehemia Cain approached the reception manager and asked in a combative tone, "May I ask if you have passed my message to Mrs. Achten?" The reception manager was completely unimpressed and said, "I did, and I will let you know when to go up." We sat and waited but Nehemia Cain was very impatient and after an hour went again to inquire. This time he received a short and formal answer: "We will let you know." Nehemia Cain told me that unless we got called up within half an hour, he would leave. I further explained that when they called us, it was not yet the actual meeting, it only meant that we could go up to the showroom where we could hang our collection, inform the reception that we were ready, and then wait for Mrs. Achten to come and look at our presentation. He asked me what the expected extent of this sale to Hertie was. I replied that should the lady be in a good mood and the price was right, and most important, if she liked the design of the collection—there was a good chance that we were talking about 4 million German marks. He looked at me and said, "That's a lot of money, it is best that she doesn't see me. I have no patience when it comes to talking to bitches." He wished me luck and left. Five minutes later my name was called. I hung the clothes by color, and Mrs. Achten came and asked in German, "Has the General left?"

We started working, and many of the garments ended up hanging on the "ordered" hanger. We finalized the prices and then she apologized for the incident the year before. I told her that, first of all, she was right, secondly, that we had been able to sell most of the skirts, and third, I proposed that we concentrate on the future and let bygones be bygones. She really liked my response. She required that before every shipment I would talk with her in person, and said she would come to Israel to inspect the quality and approve the goods for shipping.

A Proposal from Sudan

Nehemia Cain asked me to fly over to Milan for examining an Italian made computerized, automatic, and state-of-the-art spinning mill that could help Kitan cut down on manpower. Upon my arrival at the hotel, I called the company to inform them that I was coming the next day and they said it would be better to come the day after, but they were willing to have me the next day if necessary, on the condition that I didn't present myself as an Israeli. I told them I could come as a German.

A limousine driver came to pick me up the next morning, and he made sure to remind me of the identity matter. A minibus with a delegation from Sudan arrived on the same day and all of us were taken to see the machinery. We received a lot of information, but the Sudanese did not seem to understand anything—as they had no questions. Among them, there was one black man with white hair who remained by my side the whole time. During lunch time he asked the hosts to arrange for us to eat together, and the Italians took us to a different restaurant. He requested that the Italian who escorted us would give us privacy, and when we were alone, he asked me if I would have chosen to buy such a mill if I were him. I estimated that such a facility would require much high-tech maintenance and told him that they might find themselves dependent on engineering services from the Italian company for elongated periods of time, which might be problematic for them. I noted that the outcome of such a mill had no quality advantages over a conventional mill and its main benefits of saving on manpower. I assumed their best interest was to employ as many workers as possible and not to minimize the workforce. At the end of that day, he asked to talk to me. He told me that he used to be the Deputy Commander-in-Chief of Sudan's army, and that after his service, the president of Sudan, Nimeiri, put him in charge of the Sudanese Cotton industry, which was Sudan's largest export. He offered me a job paying $50,000 per month, including accommodations for the family in a large beautiful Villa and an excellent American school for the kids in Khartoum. I was a bit shocked and told him I would consult with my wife and get back to him.

I told Nehemia Cain about this offer, and he said that it sounded tempting but that Sudan was not a safe place. About a month later a coup took place in Sudan, Nimeiri fled to Cairo, and I saw on the television that 12 generals were executed by hanging—the third from the right was, unfortunately, my friend.

My next project was the Kitan stores. I visited each store and met with store managers and staff. Performance varied from store to store, but all of them had an air of "stores for the elderly," which I worked hard to change, with the new Hadar Yosef flagship store leading the way.

Rumors had it that people in Beit She'an missed the manager who had left, and as for me, I went to work very early in the morning and came home late in the evening. During the weekends, we eventually planted about 4 acres of persimmon trees, in addition to almost an acre of a citrus orchard. Edna tended to the agricultural work, and we used to joke that she was the peasant, and I was the gentleman. Life was wonderful, and I was thankful for the decision to move to Yokne'am.

Practicum Program at Wharton Business School

The Wharton Global Consulting Practicum was a program with subsidiary partnerships in Israel (Tel Aviv University) and other countries. Groups of MBA students at Wharton worked with foreign client companies on real projects to either help them succeed at marketing in the US, or help a US firm succeed in the partner's country.

Each year a handful of Israeli managers were sent to Philadelphia, studied alongside MBA students, worked with a team on a project, and co-wrote a dissertation accordingly.

Being driven to make a great success of this program, Professor Dov Pekelman and IDF's Chief Engineering Officer, Brigadier General Yerachmiel Dori, on behalf of the Israeli partners, carefully reviewed the candidates' résumés and conducted interviews to hand-pick four or five managers working in a variety of different fields. I was thrilled to have been selected. Shlomo Nehama, then a young engineer at Argaman Industries, who later became chairman of Bank Hapoalim and was almost nominated minister of finance, was also in my group with two others, a lawyer named Gideon and one more manager whose name escapes me, from the field of medical device manufacturing.

We were each allocated a comfortable room in the well-maintained dormitories and joined the faculty. We studied from 8:00 a.m. to 1:00 p.m., and then from 2:00 p.m. to 5:00 p.m., six days a week, as we would designate Saturdays for homework and further study. At first, I was overwhelmed with the vast syllabus and foreign language. I later got used to, it but it still continued to be quite a challenge.

I was teamed up with Richard, a black student from New Jersey; Jake, a Jewish student from Florida; a student from the Deep South and Dan, a student from Argentina. Our different backgrounds, Wharton being largely international, reflected in debates and difference of opinions, while we worked on our mutual project.

Our task was to create a business plan to help a foreign textile company (Israeli in our case) penetrate the American market. We had to determine things like which products to sell, penetration methods, price levels, and to calculate the prospects and the required investments. Each team member had to get to know Kitan and be able to examine questions such as Kitan's potential for penetrating the American market, whether particular geographic areas are advisable, the expected time for such penetration, or perhaps the possibility that it would be a pointless effort and a waste of time and money. When we focused on the second part of the program, it was up to me to prepare and present all the background on Kitan. The Dean, Professor Leonard Lodish, was extremely helpful, not to mention the fact that he was an outstanding human being.

Our teamwork was intensive. We held many conversations and debates, developed proposals for each product, examined whether it suited the American market or, if not, whether it could be adjusted (and if so, in what way) to fit the market. Other teams worked on different projects; for example, Gideon, the Lawyer, was from a family of winemakers and his team's task involved a lot of wine tasting, so as to conclude which wine would be a bestseller. My team and I did much of our research in the stores and marketplace, gathering information about products, prices, colors, etc. As this work was very time-consuming, I would pay for lunch, to compensate for the team's willingness to work on Saturdays. The team really liked this arrangement.

We slowly formed a direction. The team thought that dealing with fashion was too complicated, as it required four seasons every year, shipping the goods by air, and it was a risky business. In addition, we didn't think Kitan had anything special to offer the American fashion world. We, therefore, concluded that the best option was to focus on the field of bedding and we invested our time in examining that market.

One day Richard and I visited Philadelphia's largest bedding warehouse. The visit was prearranged through Wharton, so the owner-manager was expecting us. We entered his office. I was astonished to be faced with the biggest human I had ever set eyes on. He was at least 6.6 feet tall and overweight. I couldn't take my eyes off him. He sat on a huge chair by his desk and asked, in a soft high voice, how he could help. We took some time to pull ourselves together in the face of that contrast between the sheer size of this man and the childlike pitch of his voice, but we then told him about the program and about our project aiming to introduce Kitan's bedding lines into the American market. We asked if he could share his extensive experience with us, being, as we heard, one of the largest businesses in that field.

He sized us up and suddenly turned to me and asked if I spoke Yiddish. I would never have expected that giant to prove to be a Jew, but I nodded. He then asked me in Yiddish, "How come you brought this black student with you?" Richard immediately got up and left the room. I followed him only to find out that he was quite fluent in Yiddish—as growing up, he had Yiddish-speaking neighbors whose home was like a second home to him. I returned to the office and told the manager that he had offended my colleague, and we would therefore leave. He described to me a recent trauma he suffered, when two black men entered his office, pulled out a handgun and instructed him to open his safe. He said to them, "I will, just don't kill me please." He opened the safe, grabbed a loaded pistol and shot them. One of them was killed and the other injured. When the police arrived, he told me, they said to him that those two were well known and that he was extremely lucky. He then asked me to stay, but I refused and joined Richard outside. What Dean Len Lodish had to say about this story was: "That's America for you! Anti-Semitism exists, but there are also Jews who behave in a nasty way." Lodish was Jewish himself.

When we wrote our thesis, our main propositions were that Kitan should enter into a partnership with a local company, and focus, for the first two years at least, on the bedding market, flannel bedding in particular. Our secondary propositions had to do with the quality of the product. Using yarn that was thicker than usual would make it possible to brush the fabric at least six times. It might increase the production costs, but it would result in an exceptionally soft and pampering fabric. We also proposed to preshrink the fabrics through a process called Sanforization. My contribution, being the only one who had the technical knowledge, was a proposal to make sure Kitan's bed sheets would be produced from a fabric of higher quality than any material used in the American bedding industry at the time. In the aftermath, this turned out to be the core of Kitan's success in the US.

Our dissertation was very elaborate, and we included even the minutest details, such as selling Kitan's products only in sets and not as separate items. We came up with a model of a packing box from a firm transparent material that would look like a glass box, and we added cardboard divider inserts between the top and bottom sheets to maintain the package in a rigid position. We held endless discussions about each and every minute detail, and the paper ended up being my professional scripture and Kitan US business activity's "user manual." I considered the US market to be an opportunity for Kitan to expand its business, and I was even hoping that the CEO would see eye to eye with me on this matter and trust me with this job.

Upon my return to Israel, I presented Nehemia Cain with the dissertation booklet, and during our next weekly meeting he told me he had read it through and was really glad he had enrolled me in this program. I presented Zvi Tsur with a copy as well, and eventually Kitan decided to start operating in the US market.

Visit of Hertie's Purchasing Manager in Israel

In the winter of 1973, Mrs. Achten, the purchasing manager of Hertie, kept her word and came for a three-day visit. In preparation for her visit I drove to Nazareth—where Hertie's order was produced—and concurred with factory manager Beny Golsdtein to have three professionals examine the quality, not of statistical samples, but rather of each and every garment. I welcomed Mrs. Achten at the airport and a Hertie's representative took her, along with two assistants, to Nazareth. They spent an entire day checking the quality of almost all of the goods and went back to Tel Aviv, only to go back early the next day. Goldstein reported back to me that Mrs. Achten had inquired whether quality control was performed before her arrival (he confirmed it was) and was happy with the quality. I was pleased.

The next morning, I joined them in Nazareth, along with Beatrix, a German experienced and well-known model. She presented about fifty of the models, and being both beautiful and very smart, had won Mrs. Achten over. At the end of the day, the manager of the sewing workshop, and the professionals who performed the quality control received each a small present from Mrs. Achten as a token of appreciation, and furthermore, she had increased her order by 25 percent.

On our way back, I told Mrs. Achten that we were going to have dinner at my house. Edna met us at the door and welcomed her in German. During dinner, there was a phone call for Beatrix from the wife of Rabbi Goren (who was the Chief Rabbi of Israel) and, to Mrs. Achten's surprise, Beatrix told us she was taking lessons from the rabbi's wife. Outside, the night was cold and rainy, and inside by the fireplace, we had a lovely evening and a fascinating conversation that had nothing to do with the subject of fashion. When they were leaving, Edna gave Mrs. Achten a bouquet of cotton flowers that were growing in our garden. She was moved, kissed Edna, and demanded that we come visit her when we went to Germany. Beatrix told me later that Mrs. Achten described that trip to Israel as being her most meaningful and invigorating business trip ever.

A New Assignment in the US

One morning, about five months after I had entered the new world of fashion, Nehemia Cain came into my office and asked about my schedule for the next month. I told him I was going to Europe with Miri Shafir and a bunch of fashion models, to present Kitan's new collection. He nodded, so as to refrain from vocalizing his thoughts, *this guy is living the dream*, and added that he would need to discuss some things with me when I got back.

Fashion shows are considered glamorous events, and that was what I thought of them until I got acquainted with the hard labor invested in preparing them, and the tension and grief that accumulate backstage. You must take creative measures and invest a lot in getting as many buyers as possible, and the right ones, to attend. You must dedicate at least three days to rehearsing and coordinating the motion with the music. You have dressers, one for each model, and other professionals backstage, and we worked with 18 models from Israel and Europe. The buyers attending Kitan's annual fashion were very powerful and highly experienced, and any production that was not of the highest level or less than perfect could lead to harsh consequences.

We showed our collections in Amsterdam, at the Hilton Hotel; in Paris, at the Galeries Lafayette; put up the show for the top buyers in chains like Hertie and Kaufhof, in Germany and in other places. I would open the evening with a short speech followed by more details about the collection from Miri Shafir, and the show itself was about an hour long. The entire tour lasted about one month.

A week after we returned, Nehemia Cain invited me to join a series of meetings to discuss the future of the fashion department in Kitan. The discussions were long and penetrating. Kitan was progressing towards minimizing our production of fashion, and introducing imported fashion into Kitan's stores, thus cutting down the workforce. We needed to act slowly and carefully, and I agreed that this was the right course to follow. As I had told Nehemia Cain, since a lot of work and considerable sums of money were already invested in the current collection, we needed to maintain secrecy, at least for several months. Nehemia Cain agreed with me and then added casually, as if there was nothing to it, that he wanted me to join him on his coming trip to the US, and that he and Zvi Tsur wanted to act on the conclusion of my Wharton project and construct a market for Kitan in the United States.

Initial Attempts to Enter the American Market

Upon arrival in New York, we met with Shmulik Ben-Tovim—at the Israel Economic Mission—with whom Nehemia Cain was acquainted, and asked for the mission's help to introduce Kitan's products into the American market. To my surprise, Shmulik pulled out my booklet and told us that he had received it from Wharton, with a recommendation from Professor Lodish. He supported the feasibility of selling bedding and believed the paper provided excellent working directions for market penetration. He told Nehemia Cain: "Your partner did a great job. I discussed the paper with Len Lodish, and he holds it in high regard."

We left the mission with a list of addresses and phone numbers, and Nehemia Cain set up a meeting schedule. Through the following week, we met with a large number of people from the bedding sales industry in search of someone who would be thrilled to represent Kitan in the US. Nehemia Cain required a Letter of Credit for the amount of one million dollars, and that request drove away even candidates that seemed earnest and suitable. We were discouraged, but whenever Nehemia Cain asked me for my opinion my reply was, "Don't despair, you are right, we don't necessarily have to achieve instant victory."

One of our meetings was with a Jewish bedding merchant of Syrian descent. He was eager to represent Kitan but was only willing to put up a small advance of about $75,000. Nehemia Cain looked at me, and I suggested, in Yiddish, to decline. When we left, Nehemia Cain said he was glad I supported him and suggested we go to Chicago where his sister lived. We spent the weekend at his sister's home, and her daughter, who worked for Bank Hapoalim, arranged for us to meet Yari Kaplan, the manager of the Chicago branch. He was very friendly and referred us to David Lanski, the Israeli Economic Attaché. We met him the next day, and Lanski coached us through all of our moves, asked many intelligent questions, and eventually told us to contact him in three days' time.

When we left and Nehemia Cain asked for my opinion, I estimated that Mr. Lanski wished to leave the Economic Mission, find a wealthy partner, and take on the representation of Kitan in the US. I assumed he had asked for three days with the hope of recruiting a rich partner during that time. Nehemia Cain said I was good at making up stories, but that he did not believe in miracles.

The Epic Story of Jim

Further to my story of the giant who spoke Yiddish, Nehemia Cain asked me if I thought Jim would be interested in representing Kitan. I believed he might be, but I was not sure it was the right thing for Kitan. Nehemia Cain did not like my reservations, and since he was the person in charge, I set up a meeting with Jim in Philadelphia. As I expected, Nehemia Cain fell in love with him. He admired his unusual size and his childlike voice. We were invited to Jim's home and met his wife, who was a tiny woman of Japanese descent. Nehemia Cain was fascinated with the size differences and could not stop talking about how these two got along together, especially in bed. . . . We had a meeting with Jim and his lawyer at a well-known restaurant and drafted an Offering Memorandum, stipulating that, within one month, Jim would send an LC for one million dollars through the bank and then go to Israel to finalize the contract. Jim and Nehemia Cain parted with a hug. Nehemia Cain was walking on air and was thrilled with Jim, his large size, his offices, and his promise to open an LC. He noticed that I had not shared his enthusiasm. I could not pinpoint the exact reasons, but I had a gut feeling that things were not as they seemed.

We were quick to get everything done as agreed with Jim, prepared 12 samples of printed bedding, with lab results attesting for the fabric characteristics. The LC though, did not arrive. Three days short of Jim's arrival, Nehemia Cain asked me to call him. I finally got a hold of him late at night at his home number and told him that the General was worried. He asked me to let the General know that he was coming, that if the LC was not ready he would bring the amount in cash, and most important, not to worry. I quoted Jim's words to Nehemia Cain and he became even more worried.

I greeted Jim at the airport. He arrived with a tiny bag hardly large enough for a toothbrush. It was obvious he did not carry any cash with him. I took him to the hotel and the next morning brought him to Hadar Yosef. As I was showing him the samples prepared for him, Nehemia Cain stormed in and shouted at him, "Where is the money? Where is the Letter of Credit? You are a liar!" I suspected Nehemia would have beaten him up had he been a smaller man. Nehemia Cain then turned to me and said, "Get him out of my sight. Go with him to the factory in Dimona and tomorrow drive him to the airport."

We went to Dimona. Jim was not too impressed with the factories. He mounted the commercial platform scale at the factory and his weight was 530 Lb. At lunch time I took him to a Moroccan restaurant. Albert, the owner, recommended schnitzels. I ordered for Jim five orders of schnitzel with French fries, but as Jim started to eat, he asked for additional eighteen portions. Albert could only provide sixteen.

Jim asked me to take him to the Wailing Wall. It took him almost half an hour to walk the 45 yards from the car. He stood there for a long while and when he returned to the car, I could see that he was in tears. He slowly entered that car and then burst into tears. It took him a long time to calm down, and when I dropped him off at his hotel he hugged me and it felt like being held by a bear. He thanked me, and cried some more. I said a quick goodbye and left. The next morning I took him to the airport, and he flew back to the US. I thought I would never see him again in my life, but I was wrong.

That night I got a phone call from Mr. Lanski, from Chicago. I met Nehemia Cain the next morning and told him that Lanski has found for us an American business man who was interested in representing Kitan in the US and was willing to open an LC for up to four million dollars. Nehemia asked me to fly to Chicago. I was to conduct the preliminary negotiations and Nehemia Cain was to come sign the contract as soon as I gave him the green light.

I had not expected such glorious success even in my wildest dreams. David Lanski took me straight from the Chicago airport to the northern Chicago offices of Keneth Spungen. I got to know a very well-to-do and successful man who had a magnetic personality and a warm spot in his heart for all that was Jewish (we remained friends for the rest of his life). I called Nehemia Cain and he arrived two days later with Kitan's legal adviser, Miki Shacham. We took three days to draft a contract with Keneth Spungen, and we saw eye to eye as we worked out the final details. We founded the Kitan America Company with the Spungen family, and Kitan as co-owners in equal shares, to be managed by David Lanski on behalf of the Spungen family, and Shlomo Knoller on behalf of Kitan.

That evening we celebrated over dinner, and the next morning Nehemia Cain said he would wait for the LC to be ready and in the meantime spend two days with his sister's family. He told me to fly back to Israel and not to mention anything to anyone until he arrived.

Kitan America

Upon my return, I got a call from Zvi Tsur, the CEO of Clal Industries. He asked how I was doing and wanted to know what kept Nehemia Cain back in the US. He complained that Nehemia Cain was avoiding him and did not return his calls. I told him Nehemia Cain had instructed me not to say a word, and since I didn't want any trouble with him, I would keep quiet. I finally uttered, "The results are excellent, and I didn't talk to you." Zvi Tsur replied, "We never spoke. Don't worry, I know Nehemia Cain even better than you do."

Two days later Nehemia Cain arrived at Clal headquarters, straight from the airport, entered Zvi Tsur's office, and victoriously placed the Letter of Credit on his desk. Zvi Tsur read the letter calmly, said "Nice," and said no more. Nehemia Cain was disappointed with the chilly response and asked him, "Did you meet with Knoller?" Zvi Tsur replied with a question. "Did he return to Israel with you?"

From there Nehemia Cain went straight to Kitan and barged into my office. He asked me if I had a meeting with Zvi Tsur and I said I didn't. He left my office feeling I was lying to him. As for me, I resented the fact that he made sure to take all the credit for himself.

A week later I returned to Chicago, and for a month David and I worked our way through a large number of destinations. David had endless contacts, and we worked hard to create a network of reps. Keneth Spungen rented a large place with warehouses and offices, and two forklifts. We launched an advertising campaign and hired the services of a studio, to design packaging that would differentiate us from the local companies. We obtained our first orders, and Kitan America was operative.

We sold only one product—flannel bedding. This product was our forte, and our advantage, as was indicated on the package, was that the product was guaranteed not to shrink more than 2%, even after ten laundry cycles. In the American market that was considered sensational. Flannel pajamas and sheets were known to shrink, sometimes even 7-8%. Almost every American could remember pajama pants that turned knee-high after the first washing. We had in Beit She'an a large Sanforization facility for shrinking and fixing cloth. We also brushed our flannel fabrics six times, while competition only brushed three times. Although the extra processing increased our cost, it considerably improved Kitan products' quality compared with local products.

Kitan America reached one million dollars in revenue by the end of its first year, with pending large-scale orders for the next year. We put in a lot of work. Once a month I would fly back to Israel for a week, during which I would visit the factories to make sure the production process was immaculate, without any short-cuts.

The studio we used was well-known, and a young designer who had won several design prizes that year and was their upcoming talent was assigned to us. When I presented a bed sheet designed by him, with sheep patterns, during a meeting in Israel, Nehemia Cain interrupted saying, "How come you pay so much for such a doodle? We have a studio right here in Kitan that can come up with much more beautiful results." I tried to explain that we had a different target audience and that American culture was not the same as ours, but he would not listen. I realized I couldn't get through to Nehemia Cain and other local experts at the meeting. They wanted me to give this work to Kitan's studio in Israel. I ruled against it for two main reasons: because Israelis had no knowledge in American design, and because I had already signed up with the American studio for one year.

They were upset, but had to accept the fact that I called the shots.

All industry's leading producers and suppliers had headquarters in New York, with office space and lavish showrooms. About once a month, a Market Week was held for buyers from all over, to come to NY, visit showrooms, and clinch deals. We planned to set up our new headquarters right there, and I presented those plans at the next management meeting during my monthly visit. During that visit I also learned of an upcoming reshuffle that came as an utter surprise: Nehemia Cain was leaving Kitan to become Carmel Carpets' sales representative in the US, and former CFO Mordechai (Moti) was to replace him. I thought Nehemia Cain had done well as the CEO; he coped with difficult challenges and, on a personal note, he had given me a free hand and had backed me. I was sorry to see him leave.

New York Headquarters

We established the new place in Manhattan, right across the street from the New York Public Library, on Fifth Avenue. We took the entire 25th floor, turning half of the space into offices, and the rest into a state-of-the-art showroom with 15 beds dressed with a variety of patterns. The showroom was very impressive and included a very pleasant lounge where we could serve beverages and snacks and close deals with buyers.

We started the advertising campaign three months ahead, investing a lot with the hope of attracting the most prominent buyers. Our strategy involved getting editorial coverage in America's leading bedding monthly magazine and then reaching out to the buyers. David Lansky was acquainted with Arthur, the magazine's editor, and he arranged a preliminary meeting in New York. We told him about Kitan, our achievements during the first year of operating, our plans for the future, and about our new headquarters. We invited him to visit our new place, but he said he was unable to come since he was taking his 85-year-old mother to Israel to fulfill her long-life dream. I offered to take them to the Tiberias Hot Springs while they were visiting the Galilee. It sounded quite out of the ordinary, but I arranged for a night bathing. We submerged in the mineral-enriched warm water and then had dinner in our home in Yokne'am. We all thoroughly enjoyed the evening, and by the time they headed back to their hotel, it was past midnight.

Following this, Arthur and Lansky met up in New York and devised Kitan's exposure in future issues, up to the opening event. It was a great success and brought Kitan to the attention of every buyer in the bedding industry. Two weeks before the market week, we sent personalized invitations to all of the buyers. The opening event was extremely successful. We recruited a Hollywood celebrity to greet the guests, and Keneth Spungen was helpful as well. By the end of our second year, Kitan's revenues reached 16 million dollars. None of us, even in our wildest dreams, had anticipated such great success.

Cooperating with Macy's

No Israeli visiting the Big Apple has skipped a visit to Macy's, one of the most prominent department store chains in the

US. In 1980 the NY store manager was Mr. Pinazio, who was of Italian descent. His lavish office was located in an office building next to the store. He felt like—and acted as—the head of a kingdom.

I tried to arrange to meet him at least ten times, and kept "bombarding" him with samples. Most attempts were forestalled by his secretary over the phone. When I finally encountered him as he passed by me at the entrance door, he recognized me (he probably saw my picture in Arthur's magazines) and said, "Stop sending me samples. I will see you when it fits me and when I set up the meeting."

The CEO of Macy's was Jewish, and when I got word that he was going to visit Israel, I convinced the manager of the Macy's Israeli office (with whom I was acquainted) to get him to visit the Kitan factories. Finkelstein arrived in Israel along with his rabbi, who was a celebrity in the States at the time. They obtained a helicopter, flew to Kitan Dimona, and then to Nazareth. I arranged for an English speaking limousine driver to take them from the airfield to the factory. We prepared in advance a meeting room, and after showing them around, we had the meeting. We each introduced ourselves, and when it was my turn, I said I was Kitan's representative in the States, who wished to ask for his help. He wondered how he could help and I said, "Mr. Finkelstein, I want to present to you two pillowcases, one is made in a European country and the other made by Kitan. I propose to blindfold you, let you touch both pillowcases, and ask which feels more indulging and pleasant."

He was at first offended, but the rabbi convinced him to give it a try. I placed in one of his hands a pillowcase made in Nazareth, and in the other, one that was made in Portugal which I had purchased at Macy's. He said, "The one on the right is excellent and the one on the left feels like sandpaper." I begged his pardon and wondered how come the number-one American retailer was selling sandpaper from Portugal but had no high quality bed sheets made by Kitan on his shelves. The rabbi was so happy that he clapped his hands, but Finkelstein was quite upset.

Two weeks later I called Mr. Pinazio, and the secretary asked me to come over immediately. As I entered, he was on the phone hollering, "What have you done to me, I am now forced to order five 40' containers from Kitan. . . ." I was smart enough not to show the smile that hid inside me, and I later found out that Finkelstein had demanded explanations. Pinazio explained to him that Kitan goods were high priced, that he was purchasing at low prices and selling everything. Finkelstein, however, decided that Macy's could not afford to offer low-quality products. I had David finalize all the details with the relevant people at Macy's and I extended an invitation for a fully paid visit in Israel to Pinazio.

Pinazio's Visit

The visit took place in the summer of 1980. Pinazio arrived with two beautiful journalists. We booked for them a luxury hotel and first of all took them to an ethnic Yemenite restaurant and to the beach, and the next day, on an excursion. We started in Jerusalem, where we visited the Knesset and the old city, and then we continued to the Dead Sea and on to Jericho. Before we arrived in Jericho, I pulled over and told Pinazio that we were entering a danger zone so I had brought along two handguns, one for me and one for him, but that he was not to use the gun unless I called out, "Fire!" Pinazio almost fainted. He got out of the car and yelled, "I do not intend to proceed any further! Take this gun away from me or else I will not get back into the car! This is insane!" I asked, "Don't you trust me?" He didn't. The journalists were taking pictures the whole time. It took him a while to calm down and then we visited Jericho and had an outstanding meal at a great restaurant there. The next morning we went to Kitan Dimona, and that evening I took them to the airport. Before we parted, Pinazio hugged me and said, "You are insane, but I like you a lot. I will never forget Jericho . . . and when you are back in New York, remember you have a friend over at Macy's."

A month later, I brought David Lanski over to introduce him to Pinazio. As we entered the large office space, with about a hundred cubicles, the first clerk called out in excitement, "Here's the guy! Hi!" I had no idea what it was all about. They all got up and shouted towards me, "Hi, Hi." One of them showed us a journal, and I realized one of the journalists published her notes and photographs from the visit to Israel. The cover featured a picture of me handing Pinazio a gun, and him fending it off. We went into Pinazio's office, and he greeted me with a warm hug. Macy's rolled out the welcome mat for Kitan.

The Target Corporation Tender

Target Corporation is one of the largest chains, with close to 1,500 department stores (1,800 as of 2017) in the United States, and they have a lot of purchasing power. We attempted to penetrate the company, and after a year of efforts we secured a trial order of three containers, but we were not successful at becoming one of their regular suppliers. David Lansky once invited a young man from their purchasing department for a visit in Israel. I found out that he was passionate about motorcycles, so I asked him over to Yokne'am and arranged with a neighbor who owned a Harley Davidson to let him ride it for a while, which he enjoyed a lot. We also invited Target's head purchaser, a highly capable woman of color. We took her to visit each of

Kitan's factories, and I also took her to visit Jerusalem. I was telling her about the Temple and the Wailing Wall when a group of soldiers of Ethiopian descent dismounted from a minibus next to us. The buyer was curious and when I told her they were IDF soldiers, she asked with astonishment if they were Jewish. She was really excited to find out that there were people of color who were Jewish and when I asked if she wished to talk to them, she was excited. I asked the officer if any of them spoke English and it immediately started a great conversation. Before we left, the sergeant asked for her phone number. He did not receive her phone number, and we did not receive an order, but it was a pleasant experience.

A month later, we were invited to Target's headquarters in Minneapolis to discuss their tender for participation in their White Sale. I flew over to Minneapolis and met with the head buyer. She told me that participating in this project could potentially be worth about 5 million dollars for Kitan. We were required to submit 12 complete bedding packages within 15 days. Target would select 6 to participate in the tender. I flew to Israel the next day to meet with the CEO, discuss the details of carrying out such a project, determine the packaging style, and choose the patterns and prints.

I had an acquaintance who was friends with the famous Hollywood star Zsa Zsa Gábor, and I came up with an idea to produce "Come to bed with Zsa Zsa Gábor" bedding sets. The idea sounded fantastic, and Gábor was even willing, except the commission she was asking for was very high, and we got legal advice against it, so we decided to let go of this idea.

I pointed out to the new CEO that working with Target meant abiding by American standards, including a timetable that was legally binding. He gave me the green light and within three days we prepared 36 designed packages of full sets. We sent 24 of them to the New York office and kept 12 as a reference for the factory manager in Dimona, where the final packing was to take place. We presented the samples to Target right on schedule, and now we only had to wait and see if we would win the bid.

And we did. I flew over to Minneapolis to finalize the deal and sent the specifications for the first order over to Israel. It was worth one million dollars, and Target planned to place additional orders totaling five million dollars. The factories started production within two weeks.

I came to Israel before shipment, to oversee the final stages, while the first container was being packed. I went to Dimona and found the production lines to be satisfactory. Everything was according to the requirements, but when I got to the container itself and pulled out a package, it looked awful! I looked at another one, and it was the same. I opened the package and found that the cardboard divider inserts were missing. There was no room for error or shortcuts with Target. Each and every detail was agreed upon and set in the signed contract.

I rushed to the packing manager who told me it was the factory manager who instructed him not to use the dividers. I barged into the factory manager's office where he was having coffee with the CEO and asked if he had told the workers not to use the dividers. I went on to say in a harsh tone, "You know very well that we provided Target with a sample. Do you not know that this risks the entire tender? Do you realize they can sue Kitan for damages? How dare you give such an instruction?" At this point the CEO intervened, only to say to me, "I am sick and tired of your drama!" I turned around and left the room, had a glass of water, returned, and said calmly, "I am leaving now until tomorrow. I demand that you undo the packages and repack everything according to the specifications. I signed for each sample personally and should the final product deviate from the specifications; I will be forced to weigh my options."

The next morning I went back to Dimona. During the three hour drive through the Jordan Valley, I made up my mind: If, as I was hoping, they repacked as required, I would do nothing. But if they had not, I would immediately ask for a meeting with the board of Clal, including Zvi Tsur and the spokesperson, and I would resign, sending a copy of my resignation to our partners in Kitan America, David Lansky and Keneth Spungen.

Under those circumstances, I did not expect a head-on confrontation with the CEO of Kitan, who was no fool. I was also confident that I would pay the price for lashing out. When upon arrival I found the container was emptied out, and packing—exactly according to the specs—was on the way, I felt relieved, but I was also saddened because I realized my time in Kitan was running out.

From that point on, the production for Target continued smoothly and appropriately. Target invested much in media advertising, and sales were going well. Kitan obtained the orders as planned and almost all parties were content. I received many compliments from many people but hardly any kind words from Kitan's CEO. The White Sale continued for exactly thirty days throughout all of Target's 1,500 stores in the United States, and Kitan proved itself to be trustworthy, with an excellent reputation.

When the project was over, I was invited to celebrate its success over lunch with the Target's CEO and board members. The CEO gave a speech in my honor, revealing that he had entered this project with some concerns as to our ability to meet the deadlines, which were very tight, and maintain the quality. He was glad to find out we had risen to the challenge and was happy with the results. Target's head buyer gave me a valuable present as a token of appreciation and the CEO invited me to his office.

He told me of his parents, who had immigrated to the US before the war, and of the help they received from the Catholic Church that enabled them to see him through university. And then he said, "You, too, were born in Berlin." In reply to my surprise, he explained that Target could not afford to invest so much in a White Sale month without a background check, which included my American partners and me. We continued our conversation in German.

The next morning I flew back to Chicago, sent Keneth Spungen a full report, and that was the ending note of Target's White Sale project. That year was a grand one for Kitan, we lived up to our estimated revenue level of about 16-17 million dollars. But as for me, personally, I felt my status in Kitan was shaky. I was a bit concerned, though I did not expect any changes in the near future. As it turned out, expectations are not always fulfilled. I made my next trip to Israel longer as I took time off to pick the persimmons alongside Edna. With the help of twenty five Bedouin workers, we picked some 35 tons of persimmons and going back to working the land made me feel good.

Λ Change of Direction

The fruit picking took ten days, and when we shipped all the persimmons to the packing house, I went back to the office planning to return to Chicago the following week. One day the phone rang and Erwin Meltzer, who used to be the Chairman of Rogosin Enterprises, was on the line, asking to meet with me. I told him I expected to be in NY within ten days, and he said he was coming to Israel and hoped to see me at the Tel Aviv Hilton in three days. Ten years had passed since I had last seen Meltzer or heard from him, so I tried to find out what he could have wanted.

I called one of the Rogosin workers whom I knew from way back. He was thrilled to hear from me after such a long time and told me he was still working there. I asked him about the situation in Rogosin, and he said the factory was in dire straits: Several customers had rejected shipments due to quality problems; CEOs were coming and going but none had any achievements; orders were scarce; the factory operated only three days a week, and the workers had no premium and bonus plans. He said there was reasonable doubt as to the survival of the factory.

Meltzer and I agreed to meet in two weeks' time in New York. He was to come up with a detailed proposal, and I had to consider whether I would be willing to accept the challenge. First of all, I needed Edna's approval as the home and agricultural burdens were entirely on her shoulders. As for Meltzer, I knew him from my time in Rogosin when he was Chairman and I was Factory Manager. I thought salary would not be the problem as, in my experience, when Meltzer needed someone, he could be very generous. On the other hand, if he thought he could do without that person, you could not expect him to be fair. I would have to base our work relationship on proper management and on a separation of duties that was clear and contractual or else the idyllic episode would soon turn sour. As for labor relations in Rogosin, it was evident that I had to establish some new kind of workers-management relationship to prevent the worker's committee from attempting to intervene in managerial decisions. I was sure that if we set the stage correctly, I would be capable of turning Rogosin Enterprise around and bring it back to its status as a worthy company.

During that week I was preparing a full report for Motti Bar-On, the CEO of Kitan. Rumor had it that he was in search of a deputy for me. I wanted to ask him if he thought this conduct was honorable, but I never did. Upon my return to the United States, Lansky and I had dinner at an excellent restaurant and thought of ideas for developing our activity. We then went to New York for the Market Week. We had 14 beds in our showroom and while I was in Israel, David freshened up the styles and set up meetings with some 20 buyers, most of them, like Caldon and Allied Stored, of medium size. These two had about 500 stores each and they sought us out further to our project with Target. A story about Kitan with two pictures of the sheep design sheets was published in the bedding magazine, indicating that it was the most popular pattern throughout all of the United States.

End of the Road in Kitan

I had a meeting with Motti Bar-On, the CEO, who came to New York during Market Week. He expressed his views about better ways of conducting the business, and when I told him that we expected to secure about 17 million dollars in sales by the end of that year he first of all indicated that he did not find this achievement too exciting, and then he pressed on with his notion that I needed a deputy. He had already designated a man, named Ehud Lax, for this position.

At the New York office, we decided to participate in the Heimtextil Frankfurt, one of the most important exhibitions, held every January. We started working on bringing American buyers to visit us there and were busy preparing the collections for that event.

In the meantime, Erwin Meltzer called me almost every day saying, "Nu? Have you come to a decision yet?" We conducted several meetings and I also met his lawyer. I assumed things in Rogosin were getting worse and they presented me with an offer; with regard to salary and employment terms, that was hard to resist. I stipulated a strict separation of duties. The authority and jurisdiction over managerial functions would be all mine, a firm system for recording and reporting would be established, and a board meeting would take place in the factory at least once every three months. Meltzer agreed to my conditions, but I required them to be in print. We agreed to meet in Israel, when I arrived after the Frankfurt exhibition, and sign the paperwork.

The three of us, Keneth Spungen, David Lansky, and I went to the Frankfurt exhibition that lasted one week. We had a booth there and, together with Kitan's long-time German representative, we greeted buyers from the US. Ehud Lax, who was named by Motti Bar-On as my future deputy, was present at the exhibition as well. On the last night, the three of us—Keneth, David and I—went to dinner, and since I considered them to be more than just colleagues, I told them everything. They were enraged and saddened, and I felt that, once I was gone, they were probably not going to stay in Kitan America for long.

Back in Israel I met Meltzer and his lawyer at the Hilton Hotel and signed all the paperwork. I asked if anyone at Rogosin knew of my return and Meltzer said he had spread the news about a week earlier. He said people were excited and told me that some of the old-timers even wept, which made my eyes water.

The next morning at 9:00 a.m. I was on my way to the factory. The weather was glorious, and I drove slowly through the sand dunes. I remembered my first ride on that road, over 25 years earlier, and I also remembered the last time I had driven there 12 years ago. I recalled my path from a young maintenance worker to maintenance manager, production manager, purchaser of equipment worth many millions of dollars from all over the world, and then factory manager. Mr. Stern, who was the CEO at the time, chose another factory manager over me and now . . . here I am coming back as the CEO.

Taking the last turn on the road I saw ahead of me about two hundred people standing by the gate to greet me. I got out of the car and everyone surrounded me, some kissed me, hugged me, some eyes were wet with tears and many called out, "Shlomo it's good to have you back!" Tears came to my eyes as well, I called each worker by name and hugged them, it was so emotional I felt weak. Later on Meltzer told me he had never in his life seen such a sight.

I was at the office with Meltzer when the phone rang. It was the office of the workers' committee and I arranged for a meeting with them in one hour's time. Meltzer asked me what I was planning to say to them and I said I would ask for their resignation.

All of the workers' committee members, the daily rate committee as well as the monthly rate committee, greeted me and said they were glad I was back, but I told them I was not yet back. I explained that I would step in only if the committee agreed to suspend itself for two years and let me assume all powers in the coming years. I made it clear that I needed their consent in writing, that their decision must be immediate, and that if they declined, I would not take the position in Rogosin. I went back to Meltzer's office and he was astounded, but seemed pleased.

The committee called for an emergency meeting in the factory dining room with all of the workers. Eli Cohen, head of the daily rate workers' committee was the first to speak. He argued that the committee was elected to represent the workers and resigning was not an option. The head of the monthly rate workers' committee spoke after him and said, "We know Shlomo Knoller, he is the only one who can save the factory and he is our only hope. I respect him and believe we should accept his terms. The factory is doomed and will cease to exist within a few months unless he takes over." The absolute majority of workers voted in my favor. I then made a speech. It said that with the help of the workers we would soon be able to obtain orders and work a full week. I promised to keep them informed and added that each and every one should pitch in so that we could function like a large family. I thanked them all and announced I was coming back to Rogosin.

The next morning I met Motti Bar-On, Kitan's CEO, and submitted my resignation. He did not seem to be too upset about it. I offered to go to the US and bring Ehud Lax up to date with everything, but he said he would do that himself, so I collected my belongings from my office, called Lansky and Spungen to say goodbye, parted with the friends at the office and went home to Yokne'am.

It is hard to say I was exhilarated, as I knew I was heading toward very hard times in Rogosin, but I was content to be the one to part with Motti Bar-On before he had the chance to let me go. It was worth the 2 hours' drive in each direction from home to work and back.

Back to Rogosin, as its CEO

Transferring Administration to Ashdod

My first day as CEO was all talk. It seemed like everyone in Ashdod called to convey their best wishes. I then took a tour through the entire factory, talking to the workers at every workstation. It took an entire week and my main goal was to establish my view that we all had to take responsibility and we should each do our best, every person in their own field, in order to save the factory.

When I wanted to sit with the accountant, I understood that he was working in the Tel Aviv office. I was surprised to find out that Rogosin had a large office that covered an entire floor in a prestigious office building next to the Tel Aviv beach. It had 10 rooms and was occupied by 25 employees. I went there to meet the accountant and asked him to prepare a full report of all employees' roles and salaries and a floor plan of the office, and bring it with him to Ashdod the next day.

We studied the data together and I asked him to secretly figure out for me how much money we could save by moving all of the administrative activity to Ashdod. He was older than me and I did not have any previous acquaintance with him from my time in Rogosin, but I hoped he would keep our discussions discreet. He turned out to be trustworthy. When he came to Ashdod the next time, he brought all the data, and when I asked for his opinion, he said I would have to take into consideration that all of the office workers would quit, and also that I would need to find out Meltzer's view on the subject.

A month after I started, Erwin Meltzer came to visit. He was very appreciative and said that he had never dreamed it would be possible to convince an Israeli workers' committee to resign. He was very impressed by the success of my daring bet. When he asked what I had achieved so far and what were my plans for the future, I gently told him of my plan to close the Tel Aviv offices. I showed him the calculations that proved it would save a large monthly amount, and argued that managing the company from one center where the CEO, accountant general, treasurer, purchasing manager, and all other executives were located, was far more efficient. Another argument was that the Tel Aviv workers were seen as workers of a higher grade as compared to the workers from Ashdod, and they also acted as such. I felt that we should strengthen the morale of the Ashdod workers. Meltzer was silent for a while. I could tell that he was not happy but he eventually muttered, "Do as you please."

The next thing we discussed, a business trip to Africa, made him much happier. He was enthusiastic, in particular about going to Kenya. He told me that Rogosin had been unsuccessfully trying to penetrate the market in Kenya, which was very large.

I also reported to him about my visit to Alliance. I had a meeting with Livneh, the technical manager, who was my friend, and with other managers, and I expected to be able to increase their orders from Rogosin.

Erwin seemed content; however, I felt he enjoyed having the offices in Tel Aviv, only a short distance from the Hilton Hotel, where he used to stay on his visits to Israel. It seemed to me, though, that he didn't expect the change to take place within a short time.

I met with all the Tel Aviv staff a few days later, and explained to them the need to move the administrative activity to Ashdod. I offered them help in moving to Ashdod if they wanted to stay aboard, but most of them decided to resign. We hired new employees from Ashdod and the vicinity and were able to complete the transition quickly and at very low cost, and we saved large sums consequently.

The Trip to Kenya

A month later, a small delegation that included the marketing manager, the previous CEO, Haim Levit, and me flew to Kenya. I liked Levit and thought highly of him, except he was unable to deal with Erwin himself and with all of the difficulties at Rogosin. We had a visit set up at the Firestone Company, and when we got back to the hotel, I asked my colleagues for their opinion. They both thought it had gone very well as this was the first time they had been offered a lunch at the factory's visitors center, and they felt we had been treated very nicely. They were surprised to hear that I had not expected to see any business following that meeting, which I classified as bad. That evening I went up to my room early and called up an old friend of mine from Gedera, in central Israel. He had lived in Kenya for many years and had connections with some of the principal leaders of Kenya's independence movement, such as Jomo Kenyatta and Tom Mboya. I told him that I was on a business trip in Kenya, described how the meeting went and asked for his advice as to how to bring about better results and get on the right track. He arranged for a meeting with a friend of his to help me. "First of all," he said, "go to the hotel bar and purchase three bottles of the best whisky available." Within one hour, a British Architect, who used to be Nairobi's city engineer, met me in the lobby.

He was very happy to receive the whisky, listened attentively to my story, told me all I needed to know about Firestone in Kenya, and what I needed to do in order to work my way onwards.

The owners of Firestone were a man from India named Marley, a man from Israel named Abutbul, and the president of Kenya, who owned 30% of every large factory in Kenya. It was already midnight when I hurried to my room and dialed Mr. Abutbul's number. He picked up the phone and asked—in English—who was calling. I replied in Hebrew and said I was Shlomo Knoller from Yokne'am, the CEO of Rogosin in Ashdod, and that I was calling from Nairobi. He retorted, "How dare you call at such a late hour?" I used a punch line from a joke about "Jeckes" (someone calls and asks for Mr. Zelig and when told he reached Mr. Fried he apologizes for the late hour—well, never mind the Jecke replies—the phone was ringing anyways). Mr. Abutbul knew the joke—it worked. He asked what it was I wanted and after I told him about our visit, he instructed me to go back to the factory the next day, offer a good price, better lead time for supply, and a confirmation from Firestone's international headquarters that we had sales in other countries. He promised to talk to the factory manager the next morning and said that if we could abide by these three requirements, we would secure an order. He ended by saying, "Don't you dare call me so late again, and be sure I am only helping you because you are from Yokne'am."
I later found out that one of his aunts lived in Yokne'am.

The next day, on our way to the factory, I updated my colleagues about the events of the previous evening. We got written confirmation that Rogosin was supplying Firestone in Great Britain and I was sure we could come to terms regarding price and supply schedule. The negotiation was long, but we eventually got an order for one million dollars which, by the end of that year, grew to be four million dollars. My colleagues requested to celebrate the success by taking a trip to the Victoria Falls, which I confirmed.

Rogosin, a Year Later

When I started, the factory was operating in two shifts only three days a week. A year later it was working Saturday evenings through Friday afternoons. Maintenance was done during weekends, and I would personally arrive every Saturday evening to restart the factory together with my deputies Yossi Segev, who managed the Tire Fabric section, and Avi Seri who managed the Nylon Yarn section and the sales. Once a month I would travel abroad to visit customers in Yugoslavia, Italy, Germany, Zimbabwe, and South Africa.

We put together a soccer team and participated in the workplace-league. I was a center-back. One year we played against the Ashdod Port team for the championship. The game reached a point where the referee awarded us a penalty kick, and none of the players took the penalty for fear of the grave responsibility. I took it upon myself, ran towards the ball and kicked it as hard as I could. It went clear over the crossbar. The crowd was silent . . . I was put to shame. One of the national labor representatives came up to me and said, "If your workers go on strike, you certainly deserve it for missing this strike."

I attended each and every wedding and bar mitzvah celebrated by the workers' families, and I made sure the former workers' committee members would come as well, as I considered it to be an important part of good relations in the workplace.

A Trip to Reward Achievements

I set short-term goals for the first half of that year. At the Tire Fabric section—to produce and ship to customers 500 ton per month, and at the Nylon Yarn section—to manufacture continuously without stopping even for one day. I notified everybody that if we reached those goals, all the workers and their spouses would go on a trip to the Sinai Desert and the Sharm El Sheikh resort on the Red Sea. We set up a trip subcommittee that included the previous heads of the workers' committee, myself, and another executive. We distributed leaflets and got everyone involved and excited about it. During April and May, both sections achieved the goals and each of the 500 workers received a pen inscribed: "April, 500-ton Tire Fabric, Nonstop Activity."

We set forth to prepare a three-day camping trip for about a thousand people (some of them had never even been to Eilat before). It was quite a complex operation, and an advance team went to set up the trip. We located a marvelous Red Sea shore at Bir Sweir that was appropriate for setting up the camp and spent the night there on the beach. The stories and photographs we shared with everyone back at work further elevated the enthusiasm and anticipation for the upcoming trip. We all set off in busses early in the morning and when we arrived at the camp it was all set up, as the crew and kitchen truck had arrived a day earlier. Large ditches that left a rectangular table in the middle were covered with blankets and became tables to sit around. The food was served, the moon was shining over the beautiful Red Sea bay of Bir Sweir, and all that was left to do was to relish and feast our eyes.

We stayed there for three days, all of the workers who were native Israelis and people who immigrated to Israel from Georgia, Iran, Iraq, Europe, and other places. We all had a lovely time together, having food and drinks, sharing life stories, singing, swimming, and vacationing. Some of the people told me this was the best of times for them ever since arriving in Israel. The project was a tremendous success!

Unexpected Transformations

Right after the trip, I flew to the Netherlands to sign purchasing contracts of raw material. The Dutch suppliers, AKZO, wanted to raise the prices, so I called Meltzer. He told me to go back to Israel and said he would come to discuss this.

When Meltzer arrived, he met with the finance manager before the Board meeting. The results were excellent in all parameters: output, sales, yield per worker, profit per ton, etc. Everyone hailed the achievements, especially in comparison with the past. We had a lovely dinner at the Dan Tel Aviv Hotel, and then Meltzer announced that the board was going to undergo transitions.

The next day Meltzer came to Ashdod. After visiting the factory departments, we sat in my office for a talk. He started by expressing his content with the results and our work together and went on to state he must make a certain change: all raw materials would from then on have to be purchased through his company in the US, which would become Rogosin's raw materials supplier. I was left speechless. It meant, in fact, that Meltzer was going to earn a commission for every kilo of raw material, and the factory in Israel would be reduced to a labor sub-contractor. Since the price of raw materials constituted about half of the products' cost, we would have no control over profitability.

After a quiet pause he said, "It is my decision and you have no say in this, and don't forget I was the one who gave you this job and made you CEO." I asked if he regretted that, to which he immediately replied, "Not at all, you are an excellent manager, your accomplishments are far beyond any expectation I ever had, but you are naïve. I am the owner of the company, and if you are in my way, we will not be able to work together." We parted in silence and the next day he flew back to the United States.

The next week I flew to the Netherlands for a prescheduled meeting regarding raw materials with AKZO. The CEO, Wilhelm Hupie, was an old acquaintance of mine from back in the days when he used to visit Rogosin four times a year on behalf of AKZO. I knew his family and he knew mine, as he had been a guest at our house many times.

Upon arrival, I was surprised to find Meltzer there. He said hello, sat next to me and kept quiet. The Dutch raised their prices, I disagreed, but Erwin Meltzer said nothing as if he had nothing to do with the whole thing. In the evening, when we went back to the hotel, Meltzer asked about dinner arrangements, and we had dinner, with the Dutch people, as if nothing was going on. The next day we each went back home. I tried to contact DuPont as an alternative raw material supplier, but was not able to set up a meeting with them.

I realized that I was treading on dangerous ground. Later on, a telegram, listing the names of the new board members indicated that Meltzer was acting diligently towards his goal. At the end of that month I flew to Italy to tend to some technical problems, and the next morning he was there, listening, but not interfering. Ever since I became CEO, we had a habit of jogging early in the morning whenever we were together. This went on in Italy as if everything was normal.

Life in the factory went on as usual. My third year as CEO yielded excellent results, the factory had purchase orders, signed by me and by Meltzer, that were sufficient to last for quite a while, as if no changes had been made. Erwin Meltzer and I neutralized each other, but so far I was still making the decisions, and he was silent.

My work was very demanding, and living in Yokne'am, over two and a half hours' drive in each direction, meant that most mornings I woke up at five. I attended a wedding or bar mitzvah at least once a week and then stayed the night in a hotel. This difficulty, and furthermore, the volatile situation with Meltzer, had been causing me to lose the joy in my work and I decided to put an end to it soon.

Apparently, Meltzer too had had enough. He suddenly turned up in Israel and set up two board meetings—one for Monday and the second for Friday. I was invited only for the one on Friday. The first meeting was held at the office of Rogosin's CPA Kesselman & Kesselman. Meltzer told the board members that he and I did not get along, that I took actions that were against his will, and that although I was an excellent CEO, he wanted me to leave the company. He asked one of the board members to take my place, and he was told to break the news to me while offering me a golden parachute. All of the board members understood the reasoning behind this move was but none stood up to him.

The designated board member arrived in Ashdod the next day, and we had lunch at a fish restaurant. I told him that I knew what went on at the meeting the previous day and that I fully understood the situation. I then offered to stay on board for six months, work alongside him and show him how we did things, especially regarding labor relations. I also emphasized how much effort I had invested in Rogosin during the last three years and the transition that took place there. He presented the offer to me: I would continue to get full pay and benefits throughout the remaining nine months until the end of that year, I could keep the company car during this time, and would get the same bonus as I got the previous year. But I would have to leave immediately.

At first I wished to follow my heart and point out that Meltzer was the owner of only 30% of the company and that he should, therefore, explain the rationale for letting me go despite my outstanding results, but I let common sense prevail. I came to the board meeting, said my farewell, wished them all the best, and that ended another chapter in my professional life. Some of the workers wanted to go on strike over this, and others were going to make violent threats, but I asked them to let me go in piece.

Hadera Paper Ltd. – C.D. packaging Systems

A New Challenge

The time between jobs is always both interesting and stressful. This time, I had no reason to feel stress, I got my golden parachute and I could take the time to rest or travel. But, some people are born worriers, and, apparently, I am one of them. I started spreading the word that I was looking for a new position.

A company named Nilit, located in Migdal HaEmek, contacted me, but we did not see eye to eye, as I required full responsibilities and authority as CEO, but they insisted on keeping their control over finance marketing. There was another opening at a company south of Tel Aviv, but I didn't want to leave Yokne'am. Eventually, after about one month, Hadera Paper Ltd. contacted me. The meeting with the CEO, Shmuel Rotem, and the COO, Yaki Yerushalmi (we instantly hit off, as we both had been growing persimmons in our spare time), went very well. They offered me the position of CEO to one of their companies—C.D. Packaging Systems, which was under joint ownership of Hadera Paper and Carmel Container Systems, a subsidiary of Coor. Following a meeting with the president of Carmel, my appointment as CEO of C.D. Packaging Systems was finalized. The company and factory were located in Migdal HaEmek, with a marketing office in Petah Tikva.

For an entire month, they kept the lid on the decision. Yaki told me not to worry, because even if Carmel backed out, he would have another job opportunity for me. The reason for the delay was their reluctance to let the current CEO know that he was going to be replaced. I found out who he was and how he was functioning and decided to be the one to break the news to him. I went to Migdal HaEmek, checked into a hotel, called the factory, and asked for Mr. Uri Ze'evi. He took the call, and I introduced myself and said that he didn't know me, but that I had something important to tell him if he was willing to come to lunch at the hotel with me.

The man who arrived was probably a bit younger than me and seemed nice and decent. He asked me what it was that I wanted to tell him and I explained that his superiors had contacted me and had decided to hire me to take his place and that we had finalized all the details, except that they were arguing about which one of them would break the news to him. I suggested that he use this information to his advantage.

He quietly thought about it for a while and then said that he saw it coming and it had not come as a total surprise. He thanked me for giving him a heads up and offered to show me the factory, but I declined.

During my time in Ashdod, and even more so in Beit She'an, I learned much about dealing with workers from deprived areas, who were, in many cases, new immigrants under economic distress and in harsh living conditions, and yet they often treasured their dignity even more than they cared about money. The workers at C.D. Packaging Systems were better off than the workers I met when I started working in Ashdod, and they were certainly less agitated than the workers in Beit She'an. But the same principals applied in every workplace: if you treat people fairly and with respect, and if you set a good example, people will follow you.

The factory produced and sold packaging. The purpose of a package is to be both functional and appealing. I soon realized that although the factory had a studio for design, there was much left to be desired in that field, as well as in that of quality control. There were many rejections due to poor quality, and it was obvious that this was the first thing that needed to be set right.

We needed to act quickly in order to improve the design, production, and marketing, and since I was highly experienced in correcting grave situations, I could move swiftly. In a similar way to what I did in the past in Beit She'an, I put an advertisement in relevant German magazines, calling for an expert to come live in Israel. I indicated that age was not a factor and that the terms were excellent. I then went to Germany for four days to interview people. Hardy was the packaging manager at Rowenta and had just then retired, after 25 years of work. I offered him a plane ticket to come and look at the place, and after a week we signed a contract. He was highly experienced and soon enough our designs took a turn for the better, with a European style. He also constructed a quality control procedure that almost eliminated the throwaways. Instead of throwing away entire orders when mistakes occurred, we would now first print only 50 packages, present them to the customers for examination, and full production would take place only after the customers approved and signed five printed sheets.

I took Hardy with me to important customers, such as Elite, Telma, and others, and we offered them free design in exchange for orders. Within three months, C.D. Packaging Systems was an entirely different company.

Economic Growth and Development

Within a short time, the company became profitable. In 1987 we participated in the most prominent international packaging design competition (as did almost all West European design-related companies), as the winners got a lot of publicity and prestige.

We participated for the first time with five different packages. One of them won first prize, and that took us to a new place in terms of publicity and reputation. In Israel, we had a large clientele. We were the principal suppliers for Elite, supplying Elite Nazareth first, and eventually all seven factories, producing packages for wafers, chocolate, and shortbread. Due to the leap in order volume, the factory started working in two shifts. Changes were made in the marketing department as well. We designated a marketing person to Elite, for instance, who would visit their different factories regularly, examine the needs, and bring the information back to Hardy and the R&D department. They would come up with a solution for the marketing person to present to customers, and in many cases the order was sure to follow.

We worked in a similar way with Telma, one of the largest food producers. The factory manager, having realized that never a day went by without them calling him, visited them once every ten days, despite their location in Arad, in the south of Israel. In fact, all of the workers at C.D. Packaging Systems realized that they were committed to serving the marketing department.

About a year and a half into my work there, it became clear to me that we had to replace our Japanese-made Komori printing machine. It was a good and reliable machine, but could only print on small sheets, at low speed, and with a limited number of colors. It became evident that unless we obtained a new up-to-date printing machine, our chances of keeping our market share would be diminished.

At the time when C.D. Packaging Systems was established by Hadera Paper (50%) and Coor, through Carmel Container Systems (50%), the Israeli government came up with a program for supporting underprivileged areas. Producers were offered two options: to be exempt from taxation for ten years, or get an investment grant covering 30% of the company's investment in machinery. New companies were required to choose the track in advance.

The owners of C.D. Packaging Systems chose the first track, which proved a total mistake—since the company had no profits and would not have paid taxes in any case. I, therefore, wanted to switch tracks and to get a government grant for the printing machine investment. To achieve that, I needed help from a government minister, and for that I needed help from Mayor Shaul Amor.

Amor was a superb mayor, who established a successful industrial area in Migdal HaEmek, which created many jobs and turned a run-down development town into a nice place. I met with the mayor, and he set for me a meeting with Shimon Peres, who was a minister at the time, to tell him about the factory, its situation at the time when I started working there, and the developments since then. I requested the minister's help in switching options and obtaining government funding. Peres refused, saying that if he agreed, a long line of 50 other factories would soon be at his doorstep with the same request. Mayor Amor was not too worried and invited me to meet minister Ariel Sharon who was coming to Migdal HaEmek a week later.

When I entered the meeting room at the city hall, Ariel Sharon and the director of the Ministry of Economy and Industry were there. Sharon enthusiastically said:

"You are from my mother's tea party!"

"Tea and cake, mind you. . . ." I replied.

Moving on to the more serious question, I explained the factory's importance for Migdal HaEmek and said that the option change would bring in money for further investments, which were essential for the factory's survival. Sharon asked me to prepare a full written presentation and set a date to meet the director in Jerusalem. He confirmed that he was in favor of helping Migdal HaEmek, and its mayor.

We prepared a document, detailing what the money was requested for, the kind of equipment required, and the expected profits from this investment. I sent the presentation in advance and set a date for a meeting. I came with Ze'ev Fink, an American-born Jew, Harvard graduate, and a highly intelligent individual, who was the chairman of the company and also chaired Carmel.

The clerk who saw us was in charge of the Investment Center. He addressed the American chairman directly and offered us, instead, loans with moderate terms and conditions, and went on to explain why they preferred to provide such soft loans and not confirm the change of option. When it looked like he was on the brink of convincing Fink, I interrupted and said that it was I who had the last word on this. I went on to say that we were not going to be convinced and that I saw the minister's car parked outside; so, if necessary, I would not hesitate to go to his office and continue from there. I insisted on the change of tracks and not taking any loans. The meeting went on for another hour, and the bottom line was that we changed the track and received a grant of several millions. Zeev Fink was astonished and assured me this could not have happened in the US, where there are strict rules. Only in Israel are things so flexible.

Komori Corporations – Japan

The equipment we urgently wanted to buy was a printing machine. We looked at a German-made machine, which was prevalent among printers in Israel, originally designed for paper printing and converted into cardboard printing. The second option was a Japanese Komori Corporation machine. We had a medium size Komori printing machine in our Migdal HaEmek factory. It was accurate and efficient, and Komori's service was reliable. The third option was a machine made in East Germany. No one in Israel owned a machine from this company, and, at that time—six months after the fall of the Berlin Wall and the reunification of Germany—nobody in the Western world had any previous experience or information about the machine and its makers.

I assumed that a new machine was going to be expensive. We decided to thoroughly examine each of the three options technically, select a preferred option, try it by sending a 20' container with a variety of our packages, and only then discuss the price.

We were able to examine the first option in Israel, with the help of printers who owned this German-made machine that had been converted from paper to cardboard printing. Further to five different trials, we decided to abandon this option. I then met with the representatives of Komori in Liverpool, England, who helped me plan a visit to Japan. Yaki Yerushalmi, who was by then the CEO of Paper Mills, following Coor's selling of their part in

C.D. Packaging Systems, gave us the go-ahead. After forwarding all the technical details to the Japanese, I flew over to Japan with Komori's Israeli agent and with Yossi, the printing manager, who had over 30 years of experience in the printing industry.

The flight to Tokyo was extremely long and exhausting. We landed on a Sunday and the next day already met with Komori representatives. In Japan, terms such as "approximately" and "spontaneously" do not apply, everything is planned ahead and recorded. We each received a booklet specifying the places we were going to visit, people we were going to meet, what would be printed in our presence, and specifications and advantages of the machine. Everything was laid out perfectly. I sat in the lobby with Yossi and, going over the paperwork, it became clear to us how much they wanted us to purchase their machine and how much work they put into making sure we would.

We spent about one month in Japan, visited many factories in different cities, and observed some 20 printing machines at work. Every day began at 7:00 a.m. and we rode for hours at end in spick-and-span trains that were never late, not even by one minute. We were impressed by Komori's new generation machinery, undoubtedly among the best in the world.

I could not tell which one of those who accompanied us, headed the delegation. They traveled with us for over three weeks and yet I could not make anything out. In Israel, one hour with people is sufficient to figure out everything.

Back in Tokyo, we started discussing prices, and I was astounded when I heard the price. We discussed the basic price of the machinery and then the price of each accompanying equipment unit. Komori's machine had great advantages, such as its capacity for auto-cleaning after each printing process. Manual cleaning takes a lot of time and the robotic automatic cleaning in Komori's new machines improved efficiency by about 25%. I tried to lower the basic price, but they were not willing to move from their original position. Their price was justified, as they delivered full value for the money, but it was above and beyond what we could afford, and we could not justify this price to the factory owners.

After two days of negotiations, I had already figured out who headed the delegation. I approached him directly and asked for a one-on-one meeting with him. He looked at me and asked to know why. I explained that I had realized he was in charge and that I thought we could maybe find a way to talk it through before giving up on our deal. He turned to his team members, said a few words, took me to an office and said, "Go ahead; I am at your service."

A few months earlier, when I had visited Komori Liverpool, I saw him there, and I am sure he saw me. We were not introduced and didn't interact at the time, but I felt like he pretended he never saw me before. I thought it would "break the ice" if I mentioned it, but, when I did, he didn't react, and his face remained blank. I told him that the people I met in Liverpool told me who he was, and mentioned the gift basket of Israeli oranges that I had delivered to him. Again, his poker face indicated no emotion, and he remained silent. I then returned to our subject and described the situation as I saw it. I explained that I had a limited budget, noted that it might be worth their while to give us a better price in the hope of penetrating the Israeli market, and suggested that their final reply should be given to us after we returned to Israel. I said that if they didn't make the phone call to us, we would understand that a deal between us was not possible.

Planeta Print

PLANETA was the largest and most modern printing machinery producer in all of the former Soviet Bloc, selling to all of Eastern Europe, including Russia. They were not hit during the bombing that destroyed Dresden toward the end of WWII, though located not far from the city. About six months after the reunification of Germany, a Western company purchased the factory.

When we visited them, they were undergoing transitions. The CEO was from West Germany and the COO from the East. One marked change was the laying off of 3,000 employees and the fact that the remaining 1,000 workers were able to increase production. The Germans from the East had no contact with Israel and had never met any Israelis. They were curious about us, and we were interested in their stories.

Mr. Schultz, for example, was the chief engineer, who, during the communist regime, was removed from his position because his son defected to the West. He then worked as a cleaner in one of the cities' buildings until the factory was purchased by the Western company. He then got his job back, and he was our contact during our visit.

We spent two weeks in the factory, studying, examining, and discussing; finally, we concluded that we were willing to buy from them provided our list of demands was met, namely: (A) The machine supplied to us would be the same one we examined. (B) It would be built in Germany, with all electric components made by the (Western) A.E.G. Company, and all computer systems made by the (Japanese) Toshiba Company. (C) It would be tested by printing, in our presence, 5,000 meters of each pattern, on 5 different types of cardboard, supplied by us. (D) If we approved the print quality, the machine would be disassembled, sent to

Israel, and PLANETA would reassemble it there. (E) PLANETA's print manager would come to Israel for 6 months to teach the local team how to work the machine.

The C.D. Packaging Systems delegation included me, Hardy, the German packaging manager, and Yossi, the print manager. On behalf of PLANETA there were three professionals, and in addition, there was Peter, a German who married an Israeli woman and was PLANETA's agent in Israel.

Sometimes, especially when Yossi was busy in the production hall next to the machine, it seemed as if the locals forgot they were talking to an Israeli delegation, as we were all native German speakers. Peter and I had a previous incident when he requested a meeting with me several months earlier and arrived 20 minutes late blaming it on heavy traffic. I refused at the time to see him and had him set up a new meeting with my secretary. This, however, did not hold the negotiations back as he had a keen interest in making this sale, and PLANETA too was under pressure to expand its market.

We decided that if they agreed to our terms, we would finalize the technical specifications of the machines and its foundations, and then discuss the prices and payment terms. The discussions went on for one more week, as they had reservations about each demand. Peter was instrumental in convincing them it was worth their while because selling to us would open the door to selling more machines in the Israeli market. They also demanded that we would be willing to show the machine to any of their potential customers. We agreed to this, of course, pending advance notice.

Upon our return to Israel, I reported to Yaki Yerushalmi, who approved of the direction in which things were going. We proposed to hold the final discussions in Israel and, with Peter's recommendations to them, they agreed. I felt that they were going to agree to almost any term we might present, just to enter a foot in the door of the Israeli market.

About one month after our return, PLANETA's delegation came to Israel. They stayed for a week, and most of our discussions were about money issues. They agreed to all of our demands, and we signed the agreement. We set a date for the trial printing and agreed that we would pay an advance payment only after a successful trial.

Trial Printing and Assembly

About a month later we received a telegram letting us know that the machine had been assembled and was ready for the trial printing. Hardy, Yossi, and I went to Germany and found everything to be exactly as agreed. A brand new machine was set up in the production hall and the cardboard material was next to it. As soon as Yossi prepared the colors we could start printing. By the weekend we finished all of the trials and everything was to our satisfaction.

We decided to fly in professional teams from Israel to study the technical aspects of the machine, and for that purpose we booked, for one week, a hotel in a remote area that was almost vacant, as it was wintertime. There were three buildings; the hotel facilities (restaurants, bar, swimming pool, and meeting rooms) were in the middle one. We set up the Israeli mechanics, electricians, and other professionals on one side, and the PLANETA group, headed by an intelligent and authoritative woman, on the other.

On the first evening, the head of PLANETA delegation requested that we all have dinner together. Food and wine were very good and the atmosphere was lovely. At the end of the meal, the headwaiter asked who was paying and no one replied. I was shocked and the only thing I could think of was to say that we were not done yet and would continue at the bar. We ordered our drinks and then I turned to the head of the delegation and quietly told her that in the Western World it is customary for the sellers to pay, and the buyers to be invited. I said that we were going to pay many millions for the machine and therefore her company should pay for the meal and drinks.

Her reply was that she had no authority to pay. I felt sorry for her, having to call her superior in the middle of the night, but I told her she must call someone in Dresden and figure this out. She got up, and ten minutes later she came back and assured me it was all taken care of, although she hinted that it was not easy.

On the last evening I took her to dinner. The food was typically German, similar to what my grandmother used to make. We spoke about life in East Germany before and after the fall of the Berlin Wall and, to my great surprise, she said that life in the East was much better than it was in the West.

"Back then, no one was unemployed and everyone had a place to live," she said.

Whether it was a nice place or not so nice didn't matter to her as much as the fact that no families were thrown out into the street, everyone could make a living, and both education and culture were available at no cost. I asked her about freedom and her opinion was that when you can educate your children and feed them, lack of freedom does not bother you. I myself felt differently about the freedom issue, but the lady was a fanatic communist and those were her beliefs. She had a high ranking position, both in the communist party and in PLANETA, and she believed that material things were what mattered most. "The rest," she said, "would develop in time."

She asked me dozens of questions about Israel, whether everyone there was Jewish, how was life there, had I fought in the wars.... When we parted, I asked her if she would consider visiting Israel and she replied, "Perhaps."

Back in Israel, an engineering company cast the base for the machine in cement, about 38 yd. (35 m.) in length, 13 yd. (12 m.) in width, and 9 yd (8 m.) deep. Six weeks later the machine parts arrived, and a week later, 14 craftsmen followed: 8 mechanics, 2 electricians, 2 electronics technicians and 2 engineers. They set the parts in the right order, and started with the assembly work. The German workers, together with 4 Israeli workers were doing a great job. Each part was properly examined before assembled, and without any hustle or panic, they advanced quite quickly.

I spent hours watching them work, but I didn't reveal the fact that I spoke German. Whenever I asked the engineers a question, they struggled to reply in English. After three weeks when they made significant progress, I invited them all to my office for an afternoon meeting. They went back to their hotel (in one of the nearby kibbutzim), showered, and changed, and came back to the factory. Being East-Germans, they had no knowledge of Israel, and, in addition, the concept of a manager calling a meeting was new to them.

I could tell they were uneasy and I started by saying that for the last few weeks I had been watching them work, and I was really pleased. I could almost hear the sigh of relief. Their friends had warned them that it was a place of war and dangers, but here they were, everything was quiet, the kibbutz where they were staying looked like a groomed garden, and now they were being complimented for their work.

I went on to tell them that I wished to reward them with a trip. On Saturday I had arranged for a bus to pick them up after breakfast and take them to see Nazareth, where they would visit two churches, then to the Sea of Galilee and Church of the Beatitudes.

I suddenly heard one engineer ask the person next to him, why the manager wanted to show us so many churches, and at that moment I asked him in German if he had visited many churches in East-German. He was dumbfounded—actually they all were— and they asked if I was German, to which I replied that I was not, and if I understood all that they were saying, to which I replied that I did. I think they didn't sleep all of that night. After the weekend though, they came to thank me in German for a most lovely and interesting tour.

Partying with the Engineers and an Attempt on Exporting

The assembly was complete and we started the running in of the machine. We tried it with thick and with thin cardboard in a fast process and a slow one; the results were excellent.

Shortly afterwards, a kibbutz who owned a packaging factory purchased a machine that was almost identical to ours, and PLANETA eventually sold additional machines in Israel and a lot of printing equipment.

We gradually parted with the assembly team members, who were done. We held a small ceremony for the ones who went home and gave each one a present. I am sure they became lovers of Israel.

The two engineers stayed for six months and before parting with them Edna and I invited them for dinner at our house. They were surprised to find out German was also Edna's mother tongue, and they told her about the trick I played on them with the language. Edna, as honest as a proper Yecke, said, "He always does that." We had a lot of wine, and the conversation was flowing. They told us that at first they were worried about coming here but now all of the workers were eager to visit Israel again and were envious of the engineers who got to spend the longest period of time there.

I asked them about the Stasi—the East-German State Security Service. They were a bit jarred by the question and said that back home nobody would have discussed it.

One of them said that, growing up there, it was inherent in their lives. At the age of 10 you joined the communist youth movement and from there you continued as a grownup as a party member. There was no other choice. You had to be a party member to enroll in the university, to get promoted in any job; you had to report your neighbors, and it was not a question of choice. In many families, family members reported each other. They were not allowed to watch Western television programs, only privileged few were allowed to leave the country and visit Western countries, and even that, only on rare occasions.

They asked many questions about the kibbutz, the wars, the IDF, and life in Israel. They asked about Hardy, and I told them that I had offered him a contract for six months and that he had renewed it four times since. One of them even said that had he been even only half Jewish, he would have moved to Israel.

It was an extremely interesting evening both for us and for them, and at the end of that week, they went back to Germany, and so did Hardy.

The PLANETA printing machine revolutionized the factory. The production and sales increased, and C.D. Packaging Systems had become profitable. In addition, when we switched tracks, thanks to Ariel Sharon, we committed to exporting; so, this was the time to begin.

I asked Hardy to do some research for us, and then joined him on a trip throughout Germany in search of a market for our goods. After driving many kilometers and examining many possibilities, we ended up with two options. A food company that was one of the largest in Germany, which offered extremely low prices, and Deinhart, a well-known winery located near Koblenz, which was willing to accept a 20' container as a trial order, after a trial run. I thanked Hardy and returned to Israel to prepare.

I assembled a professional team, headed by the factory manager, Rechavia, stressing the importance of every detail: measurements, hue, score-line depth—all needed to be perfect. We sent half a container to Koblenz, and then Hardy and I went there for the trial run. The boxes were fed into the machine from one side, the bottles from the other, and in perfect coordination the bottles entered the box. Any problems could result in a catastrophe, shattering of bottles for example, and then the machine stopped. We failed it because we had 8 stops per 1,000 boxes, and our competition had 5.

After the trial, Hardy and I had a meeting with the production manager and he said that he really liked our print work and was, therefore, willing to try again. He gave us a video of the trial for our evaluation, and added that in his opinion, the secret was the cardboard itself which we needed to get from a specific producer located in Bremen. I thanked him for his help and two days later I already met the sales manager of the Bremen producer and ordered the first 20' container of the same cardboard used by our competitors. Over lunch, he told me that he graduated from the boarding school of Ettel Abbey. He was thrilled when I told him that Edna and I had visited the place on our last trip to Germany, and went on to tell me about the growing up there, the harsh education, all the famous athletes who learned there, and how highly its diploma was regarded. By the end of our lunch together we had become friends.

When we received the shipment, we could tell that the raw material was of better quality, we printed it and sent to Koblenz for a re-run. A month later, Hardy and I arrived in Deinhart with high hopes—a failure was not even an option in our minds.

The Trial Run at the Winery

The old winery in Koblenz was well known for its prestigious liqueur. In many homes, all over Germany, the night cap came from Deinhart's blue bottle with the red rose emblem. We were confident that, should the trial run prove better than their current packaging supplier, even if the results were equal, this would be an achievement. The video equipment was set up, the packaging on the one side and the bottles on the other, and the production manager pressed the start button. The bottles entered the box and the package made their way down the automatic packaging line to the bulk 50 boxes packaging, and into the warehouse.

The line was run at the highest speed and worked flawlessly for hours. At the end of the day we found out that our stopping rate was 2 stops per 1,000 units, less than half of our competitors. We were thrilled and celebrated at the hotel over dinner, with a drink called cherry water. I barely made it to bed that night. The next day, a second trial run took place with a similar result, and by noon we had secured an official order for 4 containers, one container per month, providing the quality remained as it was in the trial. We continued exporting to Germany and eventually reached annual sales of over $12 million, with over 7% profit margin.

We developed special packages for use in agriculture, a line that was unknown in the Israeli market before. The raw material was compressed and hardened made of non-absorbent sheets in Groningen, the Netherlands, from waste. I went to Groningen to examine the possibilities and immediately saw the potential of this material, which was light weight, non-absorbent, durable, and low priced. We printed a small quantity, bright and colorful, and made them into boxes which we presented to growers of avocado and grapes, who could wash them inside the package without harming it. We received orders from all of them, and through successful marketing during the first year, we supplied the entire quantity of packages to the large avocado packing house in Kibbutz Gan Shmuel, most of the packaging for peppers in Faran, south of the Dead Sea and on the way to Eilat, as well as part of the packaging for grapes. It was a huge achievement for C.D. Packaging Systems, but it created a problem because we ended up competing against Carmel Container Systems.

Hadera Paper was restructuring at the time, and Carmel's CEO did his best to manipulate C.D. Packaging Systems into being under the organizational authority of Carmel Container Systems. I tried to convince him that it was unnecessary, as, at the end of each year, the company transferred profits in the magnitude of one million US$ to Carmel, and in any case, I argued that the company's independence was key to its success, but to no avail.

I trust that a company should be autonomous and run according to principles of honesty, fairness, and efficiency. I worked In C.D. Packaging Systems for 10 years. When I started, the company was in bad shape and that did not deter me, but when I encountered manipulations, plotting and scheming, I decided to quit. When I moved on, the company was thriving and I had made many friends from Israel and around the world. Whenever managers leave a company that had risen to impressive professional and economic achievements during their time, they wonder what the future holds for this company. In this case, I had no doubts: "The thing that hath been, it is NOT that which shall be." I moved on, to a new industry, a new technology, but I was certain that I would always come across people who want to work for a successful company and in a prosperous factory.

CEO of Alubin

Managing Alubin Company

One month after my resignation, I became the CEO of Alubin. The company, owned by Poalim Capital Markets, was managed by those who had previously led Clal, so I felt like I was coming back home. Avigdor Kellner was the CEO of Poalim Capital Markets, and Shaul Kobrinsky was the director of its Industry Division, which Alubin was a part of. The large (about 8.5 acres) factory, located in an industrial zone on Israel's northern Mediterranean coast near Haifa Port, manufactured aluminum items, and employed 400 workers.

I found a badly managed company, less advanced compared to other businesses in the industry, with low-quality products and bad business results. The first thing I noticed was the inherent conflict resulting from producing and selling aluminum windows, while, at the same time, supplying other window producers with aluminum profiles so that Alubin's clients were also its competitors.

In addition, our windows were of very low quality, their installation was awful, and the service appalling. When it rained, complaints about water leaking due to poor installation poured in, and the only remedy available was to wait for the winter to end…. Customers often complained that company installers (10 teams, each with a company car) failed to arrive on time, causing delays. We needed to improve the products, strengthen our quality control department, and reinforce the painting and anodizing divisions. I found that there were many highly professional and valuable workers whose talents were not put to good use.

The first step I took towards dealing with all those failures was to hire an excellent business consulting company. They did a good job at analyzing Alubin, figuring out its goals, and setting up a business plan. We ran the company according to the plan for a year, but it was clear to the owners and to me that there was more to be done. Limited solutions were not enough, and an extensive change was needed.

My proposal to Shaul and Avigdor was to close down the end-product activity of the company. After 25 years of operating in a certain way, my proposal was quite revolutionary.

After closing down the window production and the installation departments and selling the cars, we were left with a much more functional and manageable company that was free of its inherent conflicts of interest. We didn't lay off anyone, and any worker who wished to stay was reassigned according to the new needs of the company. By the end of the process, the workforce was reduced by about 30%.

The process took about a year, during which time we improved the painting department, increased the anodized profiles production, and there was no decline in our sales. In the following year we were already exporting, first to England and later on to the Netherlands and Germany, the factory started working three shifts and we were selling all over Israel.

In the Palestinian Authority, we had an agent named Badria, who was located in Ramallah and had another office in Hebron. He was a distinguished figure in the West Bank area and used to come to Alubin once a month. I would meet with him, and we always ended our workday at a renowned fish restaurant in Acre. With time, we became good friends.

Twice a year, Badria would arrange a seminar for most of the Palestinian window producers, at the Hatmarim (Palm Trees) Hotel, in Acre. I would usually start the day with a professional lecture, followed by lunch, and a tour of the factory. Each visitor would get a baseball cap and a T-shirt with the company logo. Whenever I visited workshops in the West Bank with Badria, people would call out: "Alubin, we produce only with Alubin profiles." It was good business (at least two 40' containers per month) and also heartwarming.

Four years after my arrival, Alubin was an entirely different company, successful and profitable. Shaul Kobrinsky and Avigdor Kellner, from Poalim Capital Markets, played an essential role in the company's success, both by being involved and committed to the company and by supporting the unconventional course of action we took.

At the beginning of my fifth year in Alubin, there was a global surge in the prices of raw materials, which placed the company at a crossroads. Poalim Capital Markets was contemplating selling the company, which was in an excellent state, or keeping it and investing about $5 million in development (building a foundry). They received an offer from the Sahar Aluminum, owned by the Segal Family, and within a short time, the company changed hands. The buyers owned a large foundry, and purchasing Alubin turned them into a concern.

Despite their offer, I was not interested in staying, and thus, at the age of 70, I was ready for my next job. Since the Segal family had much experience and know-how in the production of aluminum profiles, I assumed it would not take them long to run the business smoothly.

Shortly after I left, Badria came to Yokne'am for a visit. After hugs and coffee, I asked what was new at Alubin and I could tell that he was upset. He told me that Mr. Segal had invited him for a meeting, and, since he was five minutes early, he knocked on the door, entered the office and sat at the desk. Segal did not greet him but rather looked up and said, "I am busy, wait for me outside and I will let you know when I am ready to receive you."

After a thirty-minute wait, the secretary invited him in, and Mr. Segal started the meeting by saying, "Look here, I am the owner of Alubin now. You are welcome to forward your orders and we will send you the goods. I am not going to take you to fish restaurants or go to dine with you in Acre. I am a busy man and I don't have time for this nonsense." Badria said that his regular visits at Alubin used to be joyful days for him. I showed him respect and friendship, which meant a lot to him. Now he was going to cut off his relationship with Segal and Alubin for good. Badria and I continued to meet and maintained our friendship for many years to come.

Managing Euro Silans in the Netherlands

Managing the Factory in the Netherlands

A month after the sale of Alubin, Shaul Kobrinsky and Avigdor Kellner presented me with an offer to move to the Netherlands and manage a company there. The company, Euro Silans, produced adhesive materials for the building construction industry. The ownership of the company was divided between Poalim Capital Markets, through Nirlat (a factory owned by Kibbutz Nir Oz), and a German company. It was managed by people from Nirlat, and it was in such desperate straits, that the German owner wanted out, and so did the Israeli owners. I thought this was just the challenge for me, where I could put to use my extensive experience. Edna and I were booked on a trip to Germany and the Netherlands for the coming week, so I gave Shaul Kobrinsky our schedule and my cellular number.

A week later, as we were on our way from Holland to Germany, Shaul called and asked me to meet someone in Germany. When he gave me the address, I said I would be there in one hour. Shaul thought I was kidding and yelled at me not to make fun of him, but I asked him if I had ever been unpunctual. An hour later, when I walked into the office, everyone seemed astonished. The participants in the meeting were Shaul, who could not believe his own eyes, two other people from Poalim Capital Markets, Mr. Pesiner, and his technical manager. It felt like I simply fell from the skies.

They were in the middle of a discussion whether to close the factory and under which conditions would they attempt to continue running it for a while further. After introductions, I looked Mr. Pesiner in the eye and asked to talk to him and his technical manager in another room for a consultation in German. They were not fluent in English, and the Israelis with whom they were discussing matters did not speak German. Under those circumstances, and given the entirely different work culture, it was quite impossible to get results.

I gave them a review of my managing experience and explained Shaul's offer. I said that I would be willing to move over to the Netherlands for several years should they choose to continue running the company, and invited them to discuss it among themselves while the other Israelis and I waited back in the meeting room for their decision.

Ten minutes later they joined us. Mr. Pesiner started by saying that it was a mistake to send this team of people who did not speak German, and that it was a pity that this man who just now arrived was not sent in the first place. He then announced that he was willing to remain in the partnership if Knoller was going to be the delegated CEO and have full powers and authority. He ended by asking to meet with me the next day in order to build a work plan for the near future.

It was 10:00 p.m. by then. I wished everybody good night and joined Edna, who was waiting for me in a hotel nearby. I told her in detail what had gone on in the meeting and she shared my excitement and was happy about the outcome. We were now facing a new challenging and fascinating adventure.

I could see the big picture. I may have seemed naïve, but in fact, I was battle-scarred and seasoned. The director attempted to make conversation with me asking about my feelings, inquiring whether I really wished to live in gray and drizzly Holland, and then, as if off hand, asked me what was the salary that Shaul had promised me. I told him Shaul had promised me nothing and he let me be. I went on touring the place, entered the production halls, talked to a few people, and found out that the top ranking worker among the locals was a man named Gidu. I asked if he knew who I was and found out that they all knew that one of us—me or the Belgian—was going to be the CEO, but, he added, it did not matter because he didn't expect the factory to last much longer. I invited Gidu to sit with me in one of the rooms, and for five hours he spilled his guts and told me what was going on in the factory, and the extent of the problems.

The next morning, Shaul arrived. I told him everything I heard and listed my terms for agreeing to take on the job. First of all, everything we previously agreed upon remained as was. It would be up to me to decide which of the kibbutz members were going to keep their jobs, and the director did not exist, as far as I was concerned. Shaul had to announce his decision without delay, that same day, and should he change his mind, I wished him luck in letting Mr. Pesiner know.

Shaul did not hesitate. He assured me that he had not changed his mind, was going to honor his word and would let everyone know that same day. That was my first day at the job—I believe "clearing the table" is always the best thing to do right at the start.

I faced many problems that required immediate solutions. I needed to find a place to live, as Edna was due to arrive within three months. I needed to come to an agreement with the bank and suppliers regarding working capital and orders. I had to prepare an action plan quickly. In short, I had no dull moments.

Shaul kept his word, and the next day everyone left. I assembled the high ranking staff, which included Gidu, the Israeli marketing manager, and maintenance manager (both from the kibbutz), the Dutch head chemist, and the logistics coordinator (the chemist's wife) who was in charge of the day-to-day operation of the factory. I explained to them (in English) that work started at 8:00 a.m. and that everyone had to be on time, that we would hold a staff meeting every Friday, and that I would not tolerate any information leaks to any external business contacts. That same day (which was a Friday) I also called a meeting with all of the workers to introduce myself.

We had about two hundred employees and a high rate of workers' turnover. Most of them were employed through an employment agency. During the first work period of each employee, the company would pay both the worker's salary and an equal amount as commission to the agency, which of course had no interest in helping us hire workers that we would want to keep.

Once a month, I would drive to Germany for a meeting with Mr. Pesiner; I sent a written report, and spoke on the phone, with Shaul—at first once a week and later on once a month.

At first, I stayed at a small hotel run by a woman of Chinese decent, in the lovely town of Hoorn, not far from the factory. Later on, I found a lovely home in Barsingerhorn, not far from Schagen. It was the third house on a farm owned by Nick, a very nice old widower, who lived in one house and his daughter and family lived in the second. We soon became friends, and Nick's son-in-law became my tennis partner.

One of the company's most pressing problems was a debt of one million euros, owed to ABN AMRO bank. We were under the supervision of the bankruptcy department of the bank. They were very strict and let us know that if there were no improvement (and indeed if things would take a turn for the worse) within six months, they would declare us insolvent. There was a slight improvement in the factory, so I had hopes that we were going to be able to improve the situation and avoid bankruptcy.

Life in the Netherlands

The village we lived in was green and beautiful. In front of our house there was a brook with fish and ducks, 80-year-old Nick tended to the large garden, which reminded us of our garden in Yokne'am. He used to have coffee with Edna almost every day. He used to dress up for the occasion as if it were a wedding ceremony, and Edna enjoyed it immensely.

The house we lived in was built during the 16th century. Inside it was completely refurbished, but on the outside, it remained in the old style. We were also friends with Peter, the principle of the town's high school, and Inga, who taught languages. She came to our house twice a week to teach us, and within six months we were fluent in Dutch.

While our private life was a sheer pleasure, life in the factory was truly harsh. Since I had no working capital, I needed to improvise for the factory to survive. In Dutch business, there are no friendships. For example, I invited the people from the bank for a visit in the factory. We thoroughly cleaned all corners of the factory, washed the cars and tidied up the place. We showed the visitors—our referent and another bank employee—the production halls, and invited them to have lunch at the factory dining room. To my question about their opinion, they replied, "Make no mistake, your hospitality and cleaning the place up, this Is all nice, but the bank needs to see a change of direction. You owe the bank a million euros, and you have four more months before we close you up and declare you bankrupt." In Israel, you can sometimes turn to a friend from the army or from school, who happens to be a CEO at the bank, but in Holland, everything is cold and precise. These were the rules, and everyone abided by them.

I established the workforce and reassigned positions and rolls. Every Friday, at the end of the workday, I held an executive staff meeting, and on the third meeting, the marketing manager failed to show up. He was a member of the kibbutz, had been working in the factory for three years, and considered it beneath him. Everyone was waiting for him. I held back at first, but after fifteen minutes, I got up and went to his office. He was sitting at his desk with a cup of coffee in his hand. I said that I had called a meeting and that everyone was waiting for him and his reply was, "You are new here, maybe you will learn, although I doubt it. In any case, I was about to make a call so don't bother me." I went over to his desk and lifted one side of it. The coffee and all of his papers were all over him and I returned to the meeting room after I kicked him flat on the floor.

Ten minutes later he arrived in the meeting room looking pretty bad and sat on the side. At the end of the meeting, after everyone had left, I told him: "You are fired. Please leave and don't come back." He got up, murmured something, and left.

The next day I got an avalanche of phone calls from kibbutz members asking for forgiveness. I told them that we were in the Netherlands where they didn't have the same forgiveness policies as we had back in Israel. When the Secretary-General of the kibbutz called, I told him the whole story and added that this man was, in any case, not efficient, especially since the marketing manager had to be an experienced local who was fluent in several of the local languages. When Shaul called to find out what had happened, he told me what I did was the right thing and that he would have done the same, except in a different modus operandi.

The marketing manager asked to meet with me one more time, so I met him outside of the factory. He was almost in tears when he requested to be allowed to stay on the payroll for three more months, which would enable him to be eligible to buy appliances at a substantial customs discount upon his return to Israel. I declined his request and never heard from him again. I nominated Gidu as marketing manager and Ron as factory manager (not before he promised not to disclose any information to anyone at the kibbutz).

On the last Friday of every month, all of the workers were invited for a meal in the factory dining room. In Holland it is not customary to serve food in the workplace. We each brought a sandwich from home, including executives, and only coffee and tea were available in the dining room. For the monthly Friday get-together, I got for everyone a five-course meal with drinks and beer, from a caterer. After we ate, I would make a speech about our last month achievements and goals for the next. I first spoke briefly in Arabic (since there were about 25 workers from Morocco) and then in Dutch. This Friday get-together was met with much enthusiasm, as the food was both good and free (which in the Netherlands is a big thing) and it made the workers feel like part of a family and as participants in the factory's achievements. They were more informed and therefore cared more. The changes in the factory were significant.

We no longer needed the services of employment agencies, as the workers recruited friends and family members. People did not wish to leave work at the factory, and this became common knowledge all over the area. I understood that this was the right time to invest in marketing.

Increase in Marketing

We targeted the Dow Corning company, whose headquarters was near Brussels, and visited their offices three times. Gidu, as a marketing manager, used to go there once a month, but we were unsuccessful in securing an order from them. Finally, they called, and arranged for a visit of their representatives. The factory was spotless; we put up a "Welcome Dow Corning" sign outside; the machines were in full capacity; the workers dressed in new work uniforms, and everything was set to impress them. They toured the production halls, spoke with workers at the machines, and inspected the warehouses, and for lunch we took them to an excellent restaurant in a forest nearby.

After lunch, we sat in the visitor's seating corner and their COO thanked us for the hospitality. He said that he had very little expectations and only agreed to come because his assistant felt sorry for Gidu, who had visited them so many times and never received an order. He was impressed with what he saw at the factory but requested an answer to one question: why we thought they should place the order with us and not with our competition, whose factory, too, was clean and tidy. I expected to be asked that, and therefore had Gidu find out for me what was the lead time of their current suppliers between order and supply—which was 18 days.

I asked the COO what was their lead time for delivery and he looked at the logistics manager who replied, "18 days." I said the quality of our product was the same and that we could shorten this time. The logistics manager said that even if we could supply within 12 days, it would not make much of a difference. I replied that we pledged to supply the merchandise within 24 hours of getting the order, or in case of weekends, an order that arrived on a Friday would be supplied on the next Monday morning. They looked at each other and said, "We will try you." We had some more schnapps, and they left. Gidu turned to me and asked if I didn't think I went too far. "We will make it." I replied.

On Friday, just as I got home, I got a call from Dow Croning to let me know that she had just sent an order for a truck load of goods. It was 5:00 p.m. I called Gidu, and within 30 minutes we were both at the office, calling in 12 of the best workers. Gidu updated them on the news and asked if they were willing to work during the weekend. We offered double the regular pay, asked them to bring a mattress, a blanket, and a change of clothes, and promised to take care of the food. They were all thrilled, especially because they realized this was a breakthrough for the factory.

I called a nearby restaurant and they came in every few hours to bring food orders. Everything was running smoothly. Gidu and I were there the whole time, taking turns in sleeping, and on Sunday we called in two forklift operators, loaded our semi-trailer truck, and two drivers took off, headed to Brussels. We all hugged like a football team after the greatest victory.

On Monday morning I wrote a full report to Shaul and to Pesiner. At noontime we received a telegram from the purchasing manager of Dow Corning with one word: "Kudos." Following this order, we got more and more orders from Dow Corning and eventually we became their main supplier for our products. For us, this represented 30% of our production, financially.

The total of our sales, three years after my arrival, was over $12 million per annum. Before that, it was about $1 million. Around

20% of our sales were to Singapore, some of which was directly transferred to China. We sold to Egypt, about 10%, through an agent who was a retired general in the Egyptian army and whom I visited in Egypt several times (since 1979, Israel has maintained a solid peace agreement with Egypt, and since 1994 also with Jordan). We sold about 30% of our production to Dow Corning, and the rest we sold in the Netherlands, to large manufacturers, wholesalers, large hardware stores and chains in the construction business. Most of our customers placed their orders for 20' containers minimum. Before my time, Euro Silans used to sell, mostly in the nearby area, individual glue boxes. The transfer into bulk quantities represented the base for the transformation. It changed the type of customers and the volume of sales.

We enjoyed our life at home, had dear friends with whom we spent time on the weekends, and the house was cozy and pleasant. When it was cold, we would turn on the underfloor heating, and during the summer I would swim in the sea (Edna found the water much too cold). We went on many trips, and once every few months we would visit Israel to spend time with our family and keep track of our farmland. I missed Israel a lot. Edna didn't miss it as much. After three years I felt I had enough. I met with Shaul, who told me that competing companies had offered Poalim Capital Markets to purchase Euro Silans. He said that, since I didn't want to continue, and since they didn't think they could find a manager who would be able to take my place, they were considering selling. He asked if I would be willing to take on the project of selling the company and offered to pay me a large sum for this service and I agreed.

I needed to act in a very discrete way to prevent problems with suppliers, customers, and even the banks. I went to Germany to meet Pesiner and decided to stay the night, so that we could continue our discussion during dinner time. Pesiner's share was

50%, and he could object if the candidates were not to his liking. He wanted to know who was in charge of the sale and I promised him that I would stay on until I found a buyer, which he approved. Also I would still stay on until he agreed to let me go. Pesiner asked if I would be willing to become his partner, without having to make an investment. I thanked him dearly but told him that I wanted to go back home, to Israel.

When I came back to the Netherlands and told Edna about the developments, she was not at all happy. As far as she was concerned, staying there a few more years would have been a great option.

I started looking into the process and consulted lawyers and notaries, since two companies from two countries shared Euro Silans and Pesiner owned the land and building and the company paid him rent. After two months, during which several companies put our feelers regarding the possibility of buying, I proposed to Pesiner that he should be the one to find his potential partners. A company that was able to take on Poalim Capital Markets' share in Euro Silans, which he considered fitting as his partners. I also suggested that we could even help the potential buyer finance the deal, through the bank.

The bank was well informed, since Euro Silans was required to provide them with a monthly report that was prepared by the CFO, and specified sales, collection, future orders, shipments, and many more details. I invited Pesiner to join my next meeting at the bank in Amsterdam, and during that meeting, the bank agreed to finance future activities, since the company was properly managed.

One day I received a message from Pesiner about a man named Dan Braven who owned a large factory in southern Holland and was going to visit the factory. Pesiner requested that we show him everything and answer all of his questions. We thoroughly cleaned the factory and the participants of the meeting included the CFO, the marketing manager, and the factory manager. He came with his son and two executives. They showered us with questions. I let the relevant professionals provide a full answer to each question. After about two hours, Dan Braven got up and said, "I am an old man and I must go to the bathroom." His looks led me to assume he was at least ten years older than me but I eventually found out he was two years younger. When I noticed he was away for over 30 minutes, I went looking for him. He was not in the bathroom, but I saw him sitting on a crate opposite the warehouse manager. I listen in on their conversation and heard him asking how many trucks we shipped this week, had anyone rejected goods, how many trucks did we send to Dow Corning, and what was our packaging method. The warehouse manager was giving him full answers. I approached and tapped his shoulder, saying, "Mr. Dan Braven our meeting is not over, and now that you have found out if we were telling the truth, are you content?"

In return, he suggested that we go for lunch. We went to an excellent restaurant by the main canal. The chef was a friend of mine, and there was a lot of good food and drinks. Dan Braven sat at the head of the table and started his statement. He said that when he considered going into business with Mr. Pesiner, he never expected to see what he saw that morning in the factory. He said that, since Mr. Knoller was going back to Israel, he wished to let his son, Simon, run the factory. He then looked at his son and said, "Simon, you will never be able to run the factory as professionally as Mr. Knoller does." He told us that he had sneaked out from the meeting because the information about the factory was too good to be true and he wanted to find out for himself. He turned to his son once more and said, "Simon, what time do you come to work every morning? 10:00 a.m., right? Do you know what time Mr. Knoller comes to work every morning? At 7:00 a.m.! This is how one should work. This factory is being run better than our own factory, and we are the largest in Europe. I want to buy this factory. You are my only son but I doubt your ability to maintain it in the same way. I have offered Mr. Knoller to stay on for one more year and teach you, and I have offered him a lot of money, but he wants to go back home to Israel." There was silence for a few minutes, and then Dan Braven got up and said thanks. I was deeply moved, and I was aware of the fact that one of the most beautiful periods of my life was over and that Edna and I were soon going to be home in Yokne'am.

A few weeks passed until the formal procedures were completed, and Dan Braven's company became a partner in Euro Silans with two goals: to take over our customers and to transfer some of the production to their factory. They paid a high price for their share in the company, and, to my great joy, I benefited from this transaction.

Managing Tadmit in Israel

Homecoming

I was glad to get back home, riding my tractor and cultivating the fields and orchards. I enjoyed growing persimmons, pecans, and citrus trees, but I missed being active in the same intensive way that I was used to be for so many years.

For a few months, I was a full-time farmer, but one day the phone rang, and the Industry Division of Bank Hapoalim was on the line. We met in Haifa, and they told me that there was a manufacturing company of aluminum windows in Caesarea, called Tadmit, which was on the brink of closing down. It owed 16 million NIS (roughly, 4M US$) to Bank Hapoalim, who was, therefore, hoping for its recovery. They wanted to know if I would be willing to become the company CEO, and if I accepted the challenge, they would halt the closure process and sign a contract with me at once.

I asked for a week to think it through. I knew the company, from my time as CEO of Alubin, and straight from the meeting went to Caesarea to find out more. I walked around and snooped. In a factory of this kind, one would always find a stock of aluminum profiles, but there was nothing in their yard. I went up to the second-floor offices and found the CFO in one of them. He remembered that I once came to demand payment on behalf of Alubin and that I had been very firm. We spoke for a while and arranged to meet the next day as well. He painted a grim picture of a company in which the owners paid rent for a building (in addition to the one we were in) but never use it; drove luxury cars, in addition to a vast fleet of cars used by the installation teams, 20 company cars in total; donated hundreds of thousands of shekels to a soccer team, and had a seat of honor in the stadium. In short, the company leadership was insanely ostentatious and poured money down the drain while accumulating huge debts.

A week later I met with the bank representatives and the CPA appointed by the bank to deal with the company. I told them that I had visited the place and my findings. They were stunned. "I assume you are not interested in the job then," the bank's representative said. "On the contrary," I replied, "I am interested, but I am asking for a much higher salary." I explained that I believed I could lead Tadmit on a new road so that the company would be able to make profits.

I worked hard as CEO of Tadmit, six days a week, twelve hours a day, and after three months, Tadmit became a normal company, the factory was already working two full shifts, and we obtained orders from significant customers, such as Solel Boneh, Danya Cebus, and more. I sold some of the cars and put a stop to the donations, and by the second half of the year, the company started to profit. I decided to stay in Tadmit for one year only, and at the end of the year I announced that I was leaving. They tried to convince me to stay one more year, but I decided that, since the company was sound, I was not interested in continuing. They threw a lovely farewell party for me and the workers even wrote a touching poem, thanking me and expressing their appreciation.

Summing up Fifty Four Years of Activity

In the year 1958, Edna and I left Kibbutz Yftach and took the first steps towards independence together. We were married a year and had no one to rely on but ourselves. There was no end to our diligence, we had capabilities, and we hoped for some luck as well. Now, in the year 2017, on our flourishing estate in Yokne'am, after 60 years of marriage, three daughters and nine grandchildren, I know we were lucky.

We started our independent life in Ramot HaShavim, Edna as a chicken coop worker and I as a metalworker. After about one year we moved to Ashdod and I worked at Rogosin Enterprise for 18 years in total (in two different periods). I started as a metalworker and equipment installer, advance to being the maintenance manager, studied while working, and became factory manager, and following 14 years elsewhere, I returned to Rogosin as CEO. In Kitan, I started as manager of the Kitan Beit She'an factory and advanced to the position of deputy general manager for fashion and clothing, managing Kitan's fashion industry and a chain of 20 stores. After studying at the Wharton Business School, I established Kitan America Company and served as its CEO.

After my time as CEO of Rogosin, I moved on to Hadera Paper as the CEO of a company called C.D. Packaging Systems, and, ten years later, to Poalim Capital Markets, as CEO of Alubin. After four years Alubin was sold and to the request of Poalim Capital Markets, I was relocated to the Netherlands as the CEO of the Euro Silans Company. Three years after the company had become extremely successful, I was instrumental in the selling of its Israeli share.

I returned home to Yokne'am with Edna, worked in the orchards, and very soon I was summoned by Bank Hapoalim to run the Tadmit Company in Caesarea, which was almost bankrupt. Hand in hand with a CPA on behalf of the court, we brought it to full capacity, and it became profitable.

For the first time in our lives, Edna and I took time off for six months and went on a trip to New Zealand, Tasmania, and Australia. But that is a whole new story.

I had managed companies, for fifty years, in Israel, the US, and in Europe, and I was more than often asked about my principles and methods as a manager, for improving the state of affairs in a company, and especially in a company that was in a bad state. I wondered whether the same principles and methods apply to all companies. My conclusion was that there were differences in the nuances, but basically, they are the same. There can be different relationships with the workers, or with the speed in which changes can be made, but the basis for a manager's conduct must be, in my opinion, taking full responsibility and full authority.

In all of my years as a manager, I strictly maintained personal integrity. Whenever I have made a promise to workers, suppliers, customers, or anyone in general, I always kept my word. Before taking measures and making changes, I always studied all aspects first and got to know the company so that I could at least analyze what caused it to arrive at a particular situation. I never believed in dealing with problems in one fell swoop. I put down all of the revision moves in writing and always consulted with any available parties, inside and outside the company. I acted according to the conclusions further to consultations. When I realized that a company needed help, I acquired help, even from a different part of the world. I did so twice. I recruited a German head of color kitchen, who spent several years working in Beit She'an building a glorious painting department, and educating the next generation of his apprentices. It was a blessing for everyone involved. In the case of C.D. Packaging Systems, it was Hardy, the packaging specialist from Rowenta, whom I had brought from Germany, and the next year we were the winners of an international design competition.

In an industrial production company, marketing and selling are the central factors for the company's success. I realized the importance of quality control but I also knew that, when you concentrate your efforts in marketing, you find out that this is where the money comes from.

Throughout all of the many years of my managing career, I always felt it was important to develop a sense of community among the workers. In all the companies I managed, I wanted the workers to feel that the company was not only a workplace but also a family. This was why I organized trips for the workers, shared meals (in the factory in Holland), started soccer teams that added to the worker's feeling of pride and played on them, and more. I believed and wished to convey the feeling that we are all in this together, in good times and in bad times, and people who are in trouble can turn to the company for help.

I strove to instill in workers the feeling that we were a family and people do not leave their families. I believed in honest and fair treatment for all workers, on all levels, at eye level and without any arrogance, and my door was always open for each and every worker. I believed a CEO must always be involved in everything that is going on in the company and talk to all its workers. The CEO cannot raise the flag of the need to save or refuse to raise the workers' wages, while coming late to work and driving a luxurious car. The CEO must set an example in diligence, hard work, and caring about the workplace. And, in the end, a CEO needs luck. Napoleon said that he would not do with great and smart generals. He wanted also generals who were lucky, and the same applies to CEOs.

Photographs

Rogosin Industries in Ashdod

Haim Zadok , Minister of Industry & Trade, Shlomo Knoller and Zvi Zilker Mayor of Ashdod (behind) during a visit at Rogosin

Minister of Industry and Trade Haim Bar-Lev, Chairman Izzy Gilad and Factory Manager Shlomo Knoller with Rogosin's Worker's Committee

Managers of ENKA Holland in a meeting with Shlomo Knoller

Gideon Patt Minister of Industry Trade and Tourism with Deputy General Manager Shlomo Knoller at a Kitan fashion show in the Tel Aviv Hilton

Loading containers for export at Alubin factory

Weaving machines for tire cord

A Planeta printing machine for packages